Performing in The Zone

To Dr. Donald Freed,

With best regards,

[signature]

Jon Gorrie

Performing in The Zone

Unleash your true performing potential!

Table of Contents

8   Acknowledgements
10   Who is this book for?
11   About this book
12   The structure of this book
14   How to use this book

15   Seven tips for getting the most out of *Performing in The Zone*

17   Foreword
21   Introduction   What is The Zone?

23   Part ONE   The Theory   See details opposite
49   Part TWO   The Techniques   See details opposite
139   Part THREE   The Programme   See details overleaf
175   Part FOUR   Digging Deeper   See details overleaf

201   Conclusion
203   Afterword

204   Appendix 1   Performance Arousal:
                     How The Zone Diagrams Were Derived
211   Appendix 2   Performance Journal

216   Bibliography and Suggested Further Reading
224   About the author

4

Part ONE   The Theory

24 Chapter 1 The alternative performance equation
28 Chapter 2 What is performance arousal?
36 Chapter 3 Why do we experience performance arousal anyway?
39 Chapter 4 How much positive performance arousal do you need?
44 Chapter 5 Why do you want to perform in The Zone?

Part TWO   The Techniques

50 Chapter 6 Introduction – Getting into The Zone
52 Chapter 7 Add Value
55 Chapter 8 Breathing
56 Chapter 9 Cue Cards
59 Chapter 10 Excessive Talk, and Silence
62 Chapter 11 $E=mc^2$
66 Chapter 12 Feign Confidence
69 Chapter 13 Free Writing
72 Chapter 14 Get a Coach
75 Chapter 15 Going Peripheral
78 Chapter 16 Keep a Balanced Life – You are more than what you do!
81 Chapter 17 Keep a Performance Journal
83 Chapter 18 Laughing Yoga
85 Chapter 19 Learn to Laugh at Yourself
86 Chapter 20 Living in The Now
90 Chapter 21 My Time and Intelligent Time Management
95 Chapter 22 Posture, Body Language and Movement
99 Chapter 23 Practise!
101 Chapter 24 Practising Performing – 5 Steps to Mastery
108 Chapter 25 Pre-Performance Rituals and Mantras
110 Chapter 26 Qi Gong – A Soft Style Martial Art
115 Chapter 27 Role models and Role Play
121 Chapter 28 Self Talk: Angels and Devils
123 Chapter 29 Self Talk: Think in the Positive
124 Chapter 30 Stay Away From Negative People
126 Chapter 31 Visualisation
133 Chapter 32 Voice Quality
137 Chapter 33 Conclusion – Five Favourites

5

Table of Contents

8	Acknowledgements		
10	Who is this book for?		
11	About this book		
12	The structure of this book		
14	How to use this book		
15	Seven tips for getting the most out of *Performing in The Zone*		
17	Foreword		
21	Introduction	What is The Zone?	
23	Part ONE	The Theory	See previous page
49	Part TWO	The Techniques	See previous page
139	Part THREE	The Programme	See details opposite
175	Part FOUR	Digging Deeper	See details opposite
201	Conclusion		
203	Afterword		
204	Appendix 1	Performance Arousal: How The Zone Diagrams Were Derived	
211	Appendix 2	Performance Journal	
216	Bibliography and Suggested Further Reading		
224	About the author		

6

Part THREE The Programme

140	Chapter 34	The 12 Week Performance Success Programme	34
144	Week 1	Getting started	wk 1
148	Week 2	Letting go	wk 2
150	Week 3	Snap Shot	wk 3
152	Week 4	Focus and flexibility	wk 4
154	Week 5	Intense Positive Visualisation	wk 5
156	Week 6	Adding value	wk 6
158	Week 7	5 Sense Visualisation, and Silence	wk 7
160	Week 8	Practising Performing - Step 1	wk 8
162	Week 9	Practising Performing - Step 2	wk 9
164	Week 10	Practising Performing - Step 3	wk 10
166	Week 11	Practising Performing - Step 4	wk 11
169	Week 12	Practising Performing - Step 5	wk 12
172	Chapter 35	The 12 Week Performance Success Programme – Self assessment	35
174	Chapter 36	What now?	36

Part FOUR Digging Deeper

176	Chapter 37	The Emotional Handbrake	37
178	Chapter 38	Diet and Exercise	38
188	Chapter 39	Traditional Chinese Medicine (TCM)	39
191	Chapter 40	Alexander Technique	40
194	Chapter 41	Neuro-Linguistic Programming (NLP)	41
197	Chapter 42	Audio Programmes	42
198	Chapter 43	Get a Personal Coach	43
199	Chapter 44	Become a Personal Coach	44
200	Chapter 45	A Final Thought...	45

Acknowledgements

This book, and indeed my journey as a performer, would not have been possible without the following people:

John (Jack) Lauderdale, my teacher and mentor, to whom I extend complete and absolute gratitude for providing me with the most amazing training as a trumpet player, as well as countless life-lessons, wishing for no reimbursement other than my success.

8

My teachers and tutors at the Royal Northern College of Music, and in particular **Howard Snell,** author of *The Trumpet – It's Practise and Performance,* the pages of which have provided countless words of advice, encouragement, inspiration and insightful information for myself and many other performers.

My teachers and tutors at Gothenburg University, The University of Auckland, and Victoria University of Wellington, and in particular **Richard Hardie,** for his support, encouragement, supervision, and invaluable advice on research, editing, and academic practises during the writing of *Mind and Body: A Theory for Understanding Levels of Musical Performance.*

Prof. Jinbo Zong M.D., for specialist advice on Traditional Chinese Medicine and personal training in medicinal Qi Gong.

Nathan Schacherer, my friend and colleague, who became my student, later applying and transferring many of my teachings on brass playing and mental training to a very different field of performance, becoming a mentor to many, as well as a major source of inspiration and knowledge for me. Thank you for constantly opening my eyes to new sources of information and inspiration.

Ionel Cristea, for diligently adopting some of my early visualisation techniques for use in his successful debut performance as a soloist with the Gothenburg Symphony Orchestra.

Acknowledgements

Marc Grue, for providing the most constructive and positive working environment imaginable during the writing of this book.

Bente Grue, for her generosity, skill, and attention to detail for the graphic design and layout of this book.

The many members of the ensembles I have had the privilege of conducting, as well as the countless other **performers** around the world I have been fortunate enough to work with.

9

All of **my students,** young and old, of mental training, music, and performing in general. You have taught me as much as I have taught you.

And finally I extend my thanks to **you,** my fellow performers, without whom this book would have no audience.

Who is this book for?

Performing in The Zone is a book designed for all performers, including:

- actors
- musicians
- public speakers
- dancers
- models
- sports-people
- entertainers
- and singers

If you are a beginner, amateur, student, or professional, then this book is for you!

About this book

The information presented to you here in *Performing in The Zone* is the culmination of 15 years of practical experience as a professional performer and teacher. During this time I've constantly been searching for effective solutions and simple answers to complex problems, maintaining efficiency and ease as top priorities.

Point and click?

In today's so-called point-and-click society, we are gradually being conditioned to expect to find the answer to any question in the time it takes to execute a few keystrokes and mouse clicks. Although certainly not without its advantages, this approach of instant gratification rarely applies when dealing with the more intimate, delicate, and complex matters of the body and mind.

11

Although far from a point-and-click approach, I've attempted to present *Performing in The Zone* in the simplest and clearest way possible in order to give you the quickest and easiest understanding of the concepts, ideas, techniques and tools contained in these pages.

More than just plain text

Performing in The Zone could have been published simply as pages upon pages of plain text, creating what is known as a passive reading experience. However, the latest research in metacognition (thinking about thinking – the study of how we learn) shows that we more quickly understand and better comprehend new information if it is presented in interesting, and novel ways. Therefore, a considerable effort has been made to convert research findings and other academic texts into more everyday language, in order to make *Performing in The Zone* interesting, engaging, and easily accessible to all.

Active reading

In addition, I've broken up the text in *Performing in The Zone* by incorporating diagrams such as this one for example…

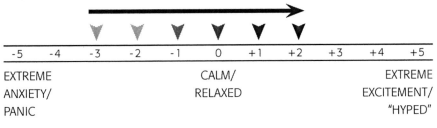

...to help explain various key concepts.

Moreover, I've further endeavoured to create an active reading experience by including a whole host of exercises for you to ponder over and complete as you read through this book. As proven by research in metacognition, looking at diagrams such as the one on the previous page, and putting pen to paper by doing written exercises when reading text can stimulate more parts of your brain than when reading passively (reading plain text alone).

12

By using this active reading strategy, the concepts, information, tools and techniques presented here in *Performing in The Zone* are made easier for you, the reader, to understand, remember, and implement.

The structure of this book

To make *Performing in The Zone* even more readily accessible, the content of the book has been divided into four main sections.

Part One: The Theory

In Part One you'll be introduced to The Alternative Performance Equation and see exactly why we all perform at different levels. The phenomenon known as performance arousal will be introduced and fully explained. You'll also discover where performance arousal comes from. You'll come to understand that performance anxiety and excitement are two different manifestations of performance arousal, and see that you need the right amount of positive performance arousal (excitement) for a specific performing situation to achieve an optimal level of performance. Finally in Part One, you'll have the chance to complete the 'What, Why and How' exercise to create motivation in your journey to optimal performance.

Part Two: The Techniques

This is where the real fun begins. In Part Two you'll have the chance to read about and experiment with more than 20 tools and techniques specifically designed to help you control your personal performance arousal level, allowing you to achieve optimal performance in your performing situations. You'll learn about Cue Cards, Role Modelling, Adding Value, how Snap Shots and Intense Positive Visualisation work, and a whole lot more.

13

Part Three: The Programme

In the programme presented in Part Three, you'll be guided through 12 weeks of constant improvement and increasing momentum, using a selection of the tools and techniques presented in Part Two. As in any good weight-training programme, you'll start off with simple exercises, gradually add weights to the bar, and build yourself up gently. At the end of the 12 weeks you'll have the opportunity to complete a self-assessment exercise, noting which techniques worked best for you. You can then repeat the programme if necessary after modifying, improving, and personalising it using the results from your self-assessment exercise.

Part Four: Digging Deeper

We are of course all different, and respond in varying ways to diverse advice, information, and stimuli. I have endeavoured to take this into account in *Performing in The Zone*, and have therefore included Part Four: Digging Deeper, which introduces and discusses some alternative sources of advice and help which you may find enlightening along your path to optimal performance. Here you'll get some basic knowledge about Traditional Chinese Medicine, Neuro-Linguistic Programming, Personal Coaching, and other exciting subjects.

How to use this book

The most common method of reading a book is to start at the beginning and follow the text through to the last page. However, *Performing in The Zone* is no ordinary book, as you can take any one of three different approaches to the information in these pages:

Approach 1: The full story

In order to gain maximum benefit from this book, and thereby a most complete understanding of what The Zone is and how to get there, it is best to read from cover to cover. In this way, you can learn about the theory in Part One, experiment with the techniques in Part Two, follow through with the programme in Part Three, and investigate some of the alternative sources of advice in Part Four if required. In addition, you can regularly check back at www.thezonebook.com where the very latest tools and techniques for achieving optimal performance will be posted as they become available.

Approach 2: The theoretical/research approach

If you are primarily looking to gain an in-depth understanding of performance arousal, Part One: The Theory, and the section Appendix 1: Performance Arousal: How The Zone Diagrams Were Derived, will be of particular interest to you. In addition, the section Bibliography and Suggested Further Reading contains many sources of information about the variety of subjects explored here in *Performing in The Zone*. These subjects include everything from the latest research in neuroscience and psychology to 5000-year-old Chinese wisdom. The majority of the sources are written in, or translated into the English language, with a few sources currently only available in Danish or Swedish.

Approach 3: The practical approach

If you are looking for practical advice which you can quickly and easily apply in your performing life, you may like to skip directly to Part Two: The Techniques. After having read and experimented with the techniques here and having completed the associated exercises, you may then choose to continue on with Part Three: The Programme. Following this, you can explore some of the alternative sources of advice in Part Four: Digging Deeper, if required. And finally, the Performance Journal in Appendix 2 is designed to be used in conjunction with the technique of Practising Performing – 5 Steps to Mastery. This technique is fully explained in Chapter 24.

Seven tips for getting the most out of Performing in The Zone

1. **SLOW DOWN.** Yes, some of us can read umpteen pages per minute. And this might be useful for getting through a novel that is 100 or so pages too long, or cramming for an exam, knowing that we're probably going to forget everything we read in a few days time.
   However, to really 'get' the information in this book, 'own' the techniques, and ultimately make the most satisfying and complete progress towards unlocking your true performing potential, take plenty of time. Stop to think about what you're reading – especially when reading about the techniques in Part Two. Think about how these techniques can be applied to you and your performing situations.

2. **Take action – do the exercises!** The exercises in *Performing in The Zone* aren't intended to be optional. They are there to engage, motivate, and stimulate your body and mind. Reading the exercises is one thing, but by moving your body, and putting pen to paper, you activate several parts of your brain at once, giving you a better chance of 'getting' it.

3. It might seem obvious, but **drink lots of water.** Why? Your brain and your body are mostly made up of it, that's why! We tend to get dehydrated before we even begin to feel thirsty. Dehydration makes our brains and bodies work less effectively, making it more difficult to understand what you're reading.

4. Is your brain trying to tell you something? There are a lot of concepts, tools, techniques, and exercises in this book. You might find yourself getting to the point where you're reading the words, but not taking in the information. You may even forget what you've read just a few seconds after having read it. If this happens, your brain is trying to tell you **"Take a short break!** I need time to process this information!" Once you've had a rest and feel refreshed, you can continue from where you left off.

5. **Talk about what you're reading to others.** Talking about what you are reading engages a different part of your brain than when only reading. If you can explain what you are reading to others, there is a better chance that the information you've read has been processed and stored in your long-term memory.

6. **Be open.** Some of the ideas, techniques and tools in *Performing in The Zone* may be totally new to you – this is good! Try them. Experiment. Find out what works for you. Remember that for a long time most of the world's population thought that the Earth was flat! New thoughts and ideas can be a positive thing!

7. **Ask questions.** Is there something that you want to find out more about? First, check the Bibliography and Suggested Further Reading section at the back of the book. Become an explorer. Still can't find what you're looking for? Or perhaps there's something you don't quite understand? Contact the email support service at www.thezonebook.com and we'll see if we can help you out.

Ready to get started? Let's go!

Foreword

In the suburbs of Auckland, New Zealand, the Summer holidays of 1991 were drawing to an end, and I was about to embark on the most amazing of journeys – although at the time I had no idea what this journey was all about, or where it was going to take me. Had someone said to me back then, "It's time for your journey to begin – time to go", my quite natural response would have been, "Go where?"

The music box

As a 13-year-old applying for my local high school – a state school with a strong performing arts department – a section of the application form seemed to jump out at me. This section contained various boxes where prospective students could indicate special interests.

For some reason I felt compelled to tick the box marked 'music', even though I didn't have an instrument and had never been fortunate enough to attend an instrumental or musical theory lesson previously in my life. For a time there was an ageing upright piano at home, but I had never shown much of a fascination for it. Mathematics and sciences had always taken centre stage up until this point. I didn't realise back then that a piano is simply mathematics and sciences – just in a more abstract form.

A journey begins

Upon starting at my high school, the students in my particular year group were divided into 3 separate classes – those that had indicated a special interest in music, those with a special interest in drama, and I assume, those who had simply decided to avoid the performance arts altogether. The students of the drama class were given specialised drama lessons each week, and went on to play leading roles in the school's rather elaborate annual musical theatre productions. The non-music, non-drama students were given extra academic tuition, and went on to become some of the top academic achievers of the school.

All of the students in my group, the music class, were told at the beginning of the year to choose a wind or percussion instrument to begin learning, so that we could with the least possible delay join the ranks of the school's symphonic wind band – an established performing group of 50 or so students from all levels across the school. Three students, including myself, were the last not to have chosen an instrument to play.

"*So, what's it going to be?*" was the question by our then enthusiastic head of music. Shoulders were shrugged accordingly, in a typical, apathetic 13 year-old manner.

"*Right, you three are going to play the trumpet.*"

"*Okay*", was the reply, and that was that. It had been decided. I didn't realise it then, but my journey had just begun.

Early success

After only one week of practising, my trumpet playing started going reasonably well. In fact things were going so well that two of the other trumpet students and I created a short arrangement of 'Rock around the Clock' (originally by 'Bill Haley and his Comets'), and performed it to our fellow classmates. The performance was a success, felt natural, easy and effortless, and most of all was a lot of fun!

I was even asked to give my first paid performance or 'gig' that same day. The job was to give the same performance in front of another music class to encourage them to start learning a wind instrument so that they too could join the school band. This time alone, I walked into the classroom in front of 20 or so students, picked up my trumpet, and performed my part of the 'Rock around the Clock' arrangement that we'd made earlier – and I didn't think twice about it.

"See! That's how easy it is! And he's only been playing for a week!"

The journey takes flight

Throughout my five years at high school I performed literally hundreds of times as a soloist, chamber musician, and principal trumpet with the school's international award-winning ensembles and toured extensively both nationally and internationally. My journey was taking flight. I had begun to see the world, and it was thanks to performing. And best of all, it was easy. I didn't even think about it – I just did it.

Something not quite right

But then things started getting a little more serious. A future career in performing as a professional trumpet player became a real possibility. I had a great teacher – one of the best. Together we worked on my preparations for auditioning at some of the prestigious conservatories in England – a country literally half a world away that in my reality had only previously existed in books, stories, and on the television. This aside, I went to a local travel agency, purchased a one-way ticket, and hoped for the best. Following the audition tour, I was fortunate enough to be accepted into performance programmes at all of my dream schools.

The auditions must've gone well given the results, but there was something that didn't feel quite right during my final preparations and the auditions themselves – something I just couldn't put my finger on. I didn't feel completely at ease. It felt uncomfortable to stand there and play for these great performers on the audition juries, despite their welcoming smiles. I felt hot in my face and ice cold in my extremities. And of course there was the torture of the pre-audition waiting time.

Anxieties under the surface

During my time as a student at my chosen performance school I appeared many times as a solo performer, chamber musician, and orchestral musician. And again, things seemed to be on the right track – there were some great reviews and encouraging comments from teachers, fellow students, audience members, and well-respected members of the classical music profession – although underlying it all, this uneasy feeling seemed to be growing.

At the time I assumed that this feeling of discomfort in performing situations was a result of external stresses. As an overseas resident, my tuition fees were almost ten times those of the local students. Without external financial support I was forced to work two jobs – one in the early morning in a kitchen and one in the evening in a bar – just to pay for my basic living costs. However, although the days were long and the situation tough, I somehow knew that there was more at play than simply financial anxieties.

A wake-up call

And then one day it happened. I was 22 years old and it was the day of an important solo recital which was to be assessed by a specialist jury. The temperature in the recital hall was high, and the air stale due to the day's previous performances. Throughout that whole morning and early afternoon I felt uneasy, uncomfortable, stressed, and far from confident – a little different to that first effortless gig as a 13 year old. With 9 years of training and literally thousands of hours of practise and performance experience under my belt, I was in worse mental shape than when I had been performing for only a week.

The recital came and went. It was an ambitious programme, and I was affected by a phenomenon that I'd later go on to know as performance arousal – a term I myself would define. The jury weren't feeling particularly charitable that day, and decided to fail myself as well as a host of other students. Due to my performance arousal level I'd not given my best performance, but I was obviously not the only one. In keeping with the policy of the school, we were all given the option of a second-chance performance at a later date.

Second chance

I had been given a few months to prepare my re-take. During this time I practised as I always had done – diligently – although I knew that my level of performance in the practise room was more than enough to achieve a good passing result. It was my level of performance under the spotlight that needed work – something I had almost no idea what to do about at the time. Fortunately though, on the second recital attempt I managed to convince the jury that my level of performance was indeed of a high enough standard to achieve a respectable passing grade.

A journey of discovery and rediscovery

Since the fateful day of that first recital attempt, I have spent literally thousands of hours researching just what goes on in the minds and bodies of both successful and unsuccessful performers, as well as trying to find out how to regain the effortlessness of my very first gig. With every subsequent performance I made, new tools and techniques were invented, tested, and improved. Gradually, steps were taken in the right direction on the road to rediscovery.

Tools and techniques that work!

It is thanks to these tools and techniques now presented to you here in *Performing in The Zone* that I have been able to give literally hundreds if not thousands of successful performances as a soloist, chamber musician, orchestral/opera musician, and public speaker, to literally hundreds of thousands of people in countries all around the world. I've been able to achieve optimal performance results in high pressure situations such as auditions, performing previously unseen works in both rehearsals and concerts, performing professionally as a soloist with uncompromising conductors, and indeed explaining and coaching the exercises and techniques in *Performing in The Zone* to some truly excellent performers.

A personal message

With the help of the theory, techniques, programme, and additional sources of help presented here in *Performing in The Zone*, I've been able to rediscover that place I was in as a 13 year old – a place where optimal performance is possible – a place I like to call The Zone. It's my sincere wish that you too, with the help of this book, will be able to reach The Zone in your field of performance.

Introduction: What is The Zone?

The Zone is intangible. It is that mind state where everything clicks, everything is easy, where your actions are effortless, and when your results are up to or even exceed your previous expectations. The Zone is quite simply being in the perfect state of mind for a given performing situation, resulting in an optimal level of performance.

We're all performers

Actors, musicians, public speakers, dancers, models, sports-people, entertainers, and singers – we all have something in common – we're all performers, and we're all in the public eye. We've all received or are possibly still receiving intensive specialised training in our particular disciplines – voice projection and resonance, scales and arpeggios, audience engagement, repertoire, diction, flexibility and strength exercises, tactics and strategy, posture and poise, the list goes on and on.

The challenge

We all strive to achieve in our chosen disciplines. However the challenge to a lot of us is that there are so few people teaching the inner art of performing. I'm not talking about how you 'look' or what you appear to be 'doing' in the performance environment, I'm talking about what is going on **inside your mind!** We are often just expected to 'know' how to perform, and this is where trouble can start.

We train, use thousands of hours of practise time, we improve, we go out into the performance environment – whether it be the stage, studio, sports field or catwalk – and we all, sooner or later, for better or for worse, get affected by the performance situation.

Performance arousal

We experience performance arousal – a phenomenon that can have positive effects by getting us into The Zone and improving our level of performance, or negative effects which can prevent us from performing to our full potential. These negative effects can be so strong that they can even make us 'crash and burn' in a performance situation. Most of us have experienced both the positive and negative effects of performance arousal, but few of us know why, or what we can do to control it. That is, until now...

Questions...

So what really is this performance arousal thing anyway? How can you better understand it? How can you control your performance arousal and use it to your advantage instead of letting it control you by turning your legs into jellyfish?

...and answers

With the descriptions and the techniques explained in this book, you too can feel comfortable, confident, and in control in your performance environment and performing situations. You'll learn the secrets of performance arousal, and how you can unlock your true potential and reach The Zone in your chosen performance arena.

Your journey

You have embarked on the most fantastic of journeys – a journey inside yourself – a journey to optimal performance – a journey to The Zone. Regardless of your performance sphere and ability level, your personal journey to The Zone continues here, with this book.

In the past you may have encountered some challenges and hurdles. It may even seem like you have wandered from the path from time to time.

However, you do know where you're going – and now with the help of this book, you have a map to get you there.

You are a performer. You have started your journey. Are you ready to see it through? Then let's keep going.

PART ONE
The Theory

1. The Alternative Performance Equation

There are successful performers and unsuccessful performers, 'winners' and 'losers', rising stars and the starry-eyed, world beaters and hopefuls, 'Idols' and 'wannabes', and all sorts of variations in between. Sometimes good performers perform badly. Sometimes bad performers perform well. What makes a good performer? What makes a poor performer? Why do we have good and bad days? And why does one person consistently outperform another, when they both appear evenly matched on paper?

A new area of study

Discovering the reasons why we perform at different levels is a relatively new area of study, pioneered in modern times by W. Timothy Gallwey with his book *The Inner Game of Tennis*. In his book, Gallwey concentrates on how to improve the performance of tennis players through psychological methods, rather than physical training.

In the 1980's Barry Green, a professional bassist with the Cincinnati Symphony Orchestra, contacted Gallwey about writing a book applying Gallwey's 'Inner Game' approaches to musical performance. Green and Gallwey subsequently published their book entitled *The Inner Game of Music*, in which the following performance equation is presented to account for the relative success of a performing situation[1]:

$$P = p - i$$

In this equation:

P   Big letter '*P*' is your level of performance – *how you actually perform*
p   Small letter '*p*' is your potential – *your best possible performance level*
i   Small letter '*i*' is your capacity to interfere with your potential
     – *negative thoughts, nerves, getting in your own way or 'thinking too much' etc.*

In other words, your level of performance '*P*' - how you actually perform in a real performance situation - is a result of your potential '*p*', minus the extent to which you interfere with your potential '*i*'.

For the purposes of the Inner Game approach, this equation works well, and has provided inspiration for many performers.

---

1 Barry Green and W. Timothy Gallwey, The Inner Game of Music, (London: Pan Books, 1986), 23.

Building on Green and Gallwey's equation, we can look at your resulting level of performance in a different way, by using four basic variables. These variables are:

c   **Your cognitive attributes** – *or your performance intelligence*
   i.e. the knowledge you have about your field of performance
p   **Your physical attributes** – *or physical capacity to carry out your performance intelligence*
e   **External interference** – *events beyond your control*
a   **Performance arousal** – *your state of mind before, and/or during a performance*

When put together, these variables form The Alternative Performance Equation.

The Alternative Performance Equation

$$RLP = (c + p - e) + a$$

Now, I understand that maybe one of the reasons you became a performer was so that you could leave algebra far behind you, but bear with me for just a minute!

This equation shows that your resulting level of performance 'RLP' - how you actually end up performing - is equal to the sum of your cognitive attributes 'c', plus your physical attributes 'p', minus external interference 'e', plus the appropriateness of your performance arousal level 'a' for the given performing situation. These variables are intended to have relative, rather than numerical values.

Cognitive attributes – 'c'
Your performance intelligence

Understanding scale patterns, memorising your lines, knowing the repertoire, knowing the steps, understanding the rules and tactics of your game, reading the notes, knowing how to use the equipment, knowing the fingerings – these are all examples of cognitive attributes 'c' – attributes that you can improve by employing traditional learning methods. Talent, personality, and motivation also come under the heading of cognitive attributes. In The Alternative Performance Equation, cognitive attributes 'c' always give a positive value. In other words, the 'smarter' you are in your field of performance, the higher your resulting level of performance.

Physical attributes – *'p'*

Your physical capacity to carry out your performance intelligence

Strength, flexibility, posture, co-ordination and speed – these are examples of physical attributes 'p', which can be trained. In The Alternative Performance Equation, physical attributes 'p' always give a positive value. In other words, the better your physical ability in your field of performance, the higher your resulting level of performance.

External interference – *'e'*

Events beyond your control

External interference 'e', can take the form of mobile phones ringing just before you take that final birdie putt on the 18th, a broken stiletto during the fashion show, a sticky key during the slow movement of the concerto, feedback from the PA system, a flat tyre during a cycle race, power cuts and so on. These are examples of events that when they occur, are completely beyond your control, and can have a negative effect on you and your performance. In The Alternative Performance Equation, external interference 'e' always creates a lower value for your resulting level of performance. In other words, the more affected you are by external interference, the lower your resulting level of performance.

Appropriateness of your performance arousal level – *'a'*

Your state of mind before, and/or during a performance.
This can have a positive or negative effect on how you perform.

Now we come to the aspect of The Alternative Performance Equation which is the focus of this book – the variable which governs whether you perform in The Zone or not. This variable is labelled 'a' – the appropriateness of your performance arousal level, and is perhaps the most complex part of The Alternative Performance Equation.

Performance arousal - different effects

The value for 'a' in The Alternative Performance Equation can be either positive or negative, depending upon your state of mind before and/or during your performance, and how appropriate this state of mind is for your particular performing situation. Because it can be positive or negative, the appropriateness of your performance arousal level 'a' can have either a positive or negative effect on your resulting level of performance. In other words, if your state of mind (performance arousal level) is appropriate for a particular performing situation, the value for 'a' in The Alternative Performance Equation will be positive, and your resulting level of performance will be higher.

If your state of mind (performance arousal level) is inappropriate for a particular performing situation, the value for 'a' in The Alternative Performance Equation will be negative, and your resulting level of performance will be lower.

Understanding what performance arousal is, how it affects you as a performer, and the amount of performance arousal you need for your particular performing situation, are the fundamentals of understanding what The Zone is, and how to get there. In the following chapter, we'll take a closer look at performance arousal, and how it can affect you positively or negatively in performing situations.

27

2. What is performance arousal?

The word 'performance' can be defined as carrying out a specific action or actions in front of an audience. The term 'arousal' here refers to your level of physiological and psychological activation that can vary from deep sleep to extreme anxiety or excitement. The amount of 'arousal' you experience and how you experience it is determined by your state of mind. The effects of 'arousal' can be felt in your body and mind. So, the complete term **performance arousal** describes **your state of mind before and/or during a performance.**

Excitement or anxiety

Performance arousal can be manifested either **positively as excitement,** or **negatively as anxiety,** and is a phenomenon that can be experienced by performers of all disciplines, in both private and public performance environments.

Performance Arousal can be . . .

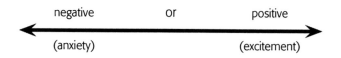

negative	or	positive
(anxiety)		(excitement)

Strong or mild

The amount of performance arousal you experience can be strong or mild. If you're not experiencing performance arousal at all, it can be said that you are calm, or relaxed – perhaps even in a meditative state.

Performance Arousal can be . . .

NEGATIVE and STRONG	NEGATIVE and MILD	POSITIVE and MILD	POSITIVE and STRONG

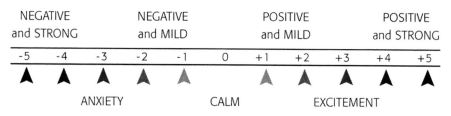

-5	-4	-3	-2	-1	0	+1	+2	+3	+4	+5

ANXIETY	CALM	EXCITEMENT

Performance Arousal Simplified

1. Performance arousal is the excitement or anxiety you can feel before and/or during a performance.
2. Performance arousal can be strong or mild.
3. Performance arousal can affect you mentally and/or physically.

Chapter 2

2a. Exercise: Performance Arousal
True or False

Q.1.   Performance arousal is not only performance anxiety.   True / False

Q.2.   Performance arousal can be manifested positively as
       excitement, or negatively as performance anxiety.   True / False

Q.3.   Performance arousal can be strong or mild.   True / False

Q.4.   Performance arousal can affect you physically and/or mentally.   True / False

Q.5.   Performance anxiety is a negative form of performance arousal.   True / False

Q.6.   Being excited about, or looking forward to a performance,
       is a positive form of performance arousal.   True / False

Solution overleaf.

Appropriate and inappropriate positive performance arousal - excitement

When you experience performance arousal positively as excitement, it is possible to reach a higher level of performance than you would otherwise achieve in your practise environment. BUT...this is only true as long as the amount of positive performance arousal (excitement) you experience is the same as, or close to the amount required for your given performance situation. In this case, the variable '*a*' in The Alternative Performance Equation is positive, and your resulting level of performance is higher.

When Performance Arousal Required is the same as, or almost the same as Performance Arousal Experienced, as in this diagram . . .

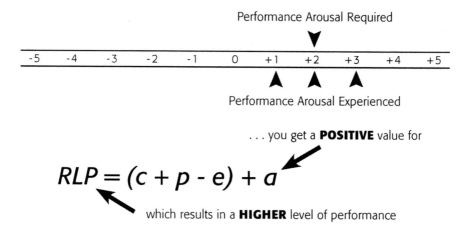

Performance Arousal Required

| -5 | -4 | -3 | -2 | -1 | 0 | +1 | +2 | +3 | +4 | +5 |

Performance Arousal Experienced

. . . you get a **POSITIVE** value for

$$RLP = (c + p - e) + a$$

which results in a **HIGHER** level of performance

This is because the performance arousal level experienced is **appropriate** for this performing situation!

However, if you are too excited about a coming performance ('over-hyped'), your high level of performance arousal can make you feel out of control. This can in turn have a negative effect on your performance. In this case, the variable '*a*' in The Alternative Performance Equation is negative.

Solution: Performance Arousal True or False

All answers are TRUE!

When Performance Arousal Required is much lower than Performance Arousal Experienced, as in this diagram...

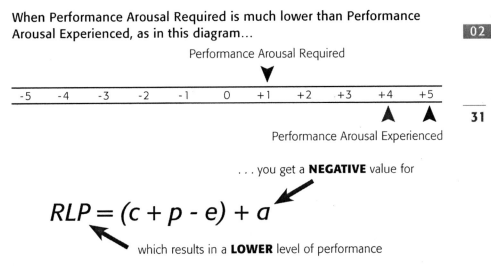

Performance Arousal Required

| -5 | -4 | -3 | -2 | -1 | 0 | +1 | +2 | +3 | +4 | +5 |

Performance Arousal Experienced

. . . you get a **NEGATIVE** value for

$$RLP = (c + p - e) + a$$

which results in a **LOWER** level of performance

This is because the performance arousal level experienced is **inappropriate** for this performing situation!

Likewise, if you're not 'hyped-up enough' for a high-energy performance, your low level of performance arousal ('under-excitement') can result in your performance being dull or boring. In this case, the variable '*a*' in The Alternative Performance Equation is also negative, creating a negative effect on your resulting level of performance.

When Performance Arousal Required is much higher than Performance Arousal Experienced, as in this diagram...

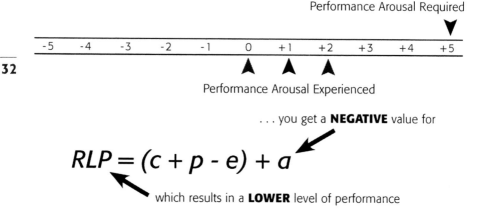

Performance Arousal Required

| -5 | -4 | -3 | -2 | -1 | 0 | +1 | +2 | +3 | +4 | +5 |

Performance Arousal Experienced

. . . you get a **NEGATIVE** value for

$$RLP = (c + p - e) + a$$

which results in a **LOWER** level of performance

This is because the performance arousal level experienced is **inappropriate** for this performing situation!

What do Professional Wrestlers and Chess Champions have in common?

We can see a concrete example of appropriate and inappropriate positive performance arousal (excitement) if we compare the level of performance arousal required for chess champions with the level required for professional wrestlers.

Good for professional wrestling...

Running into the performance arena, jumping up to the top rope of the wrestling ring, and calling out to the crowd are ways for a professional wrestler to 'psych themselves up' before and during a match. These actions can create a strong amount of positive performance arousal which is beneficial for the professional wrestler, because a high level of excitement is appropriate for this intensely physical performing situation.

...but not good for chess!

However, in the case of a chess champion about to begin a public tournament, running into the performance arena, jumping up on tables and calling out to the audience can have a negative effect on the chess champion's ability to perform. This is because such a high level of positive performance arousal (excitement) is inappropriate for a competitive chess situation where intense mental focus, concentration, and calm are required!

Good for professional wrestling, but not good for chess!

-5	-4	-3	-2	-1	0	+1	+2	+3	+4	+5

▲

Performance Arousal Experienced

Good for chess...

At the other extreme, relaxation exercises can bring high levels of positive performance arousal (excitement) to a lower, calmer level. This low activation level can be of great benefit to chess players, allowing them to concentrate on planning and predicting patterns and moves.

...but not good for professional wrestling!

However if these same relaxation exercises were to be carried out by a professional wrestler just before starting a match, it is unlikely that they would be in the right mental state to attack and defend against a crazed 150kg opponent!

Good for chess, but not good for professional wrestling!

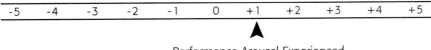

-5	-4	-3	-2	-1	0	+1	+2	+3	+4	+5

▲

Performance Arousal Experienced

As you can see from these examples, it is important that the level of performance arousal you experience is appropriate for your specific performing situations.

Anxiety

When performance arousal is manifested negatively, it is commonly given the label 'performance anxiety'. Performance anxiety can be experienced by all performers, but especially amongst those requiring precise control of fine motor skills, such as golfers, archers or classical musicians. When performance arousal is manifested negatively (as anxiety), symptoms such as nausea, shaking hands, sweaty palms, muscle tension, cold extremities, and hyperventilation may occur. The extent to which these symptoms occur is proportional to the amount of negative performance arousal experienced.

If performance arousal is experienced negatively as anxiety, the variable 'a' in The Alternative Performance Equation will be negative. And this by the way is the only thing Chess Champions and Professional Wrestlers have in common when it comes to performance arousal!

When Performance Arousal is experienced negatively as anxiety, as in this diagram...

Not good for chess, professional wrestling or any other performance situation!

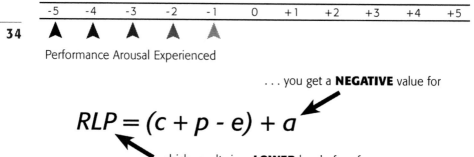

Performance Arousal Experienced

... you get a **NEGATIVE** value for

$$RLP = (c + p - e) + a$$

which results in a **LOWER** level of performance

This is because negative performance arousal (anxiety) always has a negative effect on performance!

To sum up

The term performance arousal describes a state of mind which can create psychological and physical sensations that you as a performer can experience before and at times during a performance. These sensations can be felt:

- **Positively, as excitement,** and at an **appropriate** level for your performance situation, raising your level of performance

- **Positively, as excitement,** but at an **inappropriate** level for your performance situation, lowering your level of performance

- **Negatively, as anxiety, lowering** your level of performance

The phenomenon of performance arousal is a very important aspect of performing which can affect you positively or negatively. Some performers naturally achieve an ideal level of performance arousal for their performing situations whereas others must learn to control it. When the right techniques are applied, performance arousal can be harnessed and made to work for you, optimising and even improving your level of performance in any performing situation.

2b. Exercise: Performance Arousal Multi-Choice

Q.1. Performance arousal is:
a) The excitement or anxiety you can feel before, and/or during a performance.
b) Something which should only be talked about after dark
c) Banana   Your answer: _____

Q.2. Performance arousal can affect you:
a) Positively or negatively
b) If you are an inanimate object
c) Fish   Your answer: _____

Q.3. Performance arousal can be:
a) An ingredient in soups
b) Strong or mild
c) Chair   Your answer: _____

Q.4. If you experience anxiety, it can:
a) Raise your level of performance
b) Lower your level of performance
c) Bicycle   Your answer: _____

Q.5. If you experience excitement, but at an inappropriate level for your performing situation, your performance level can be:
a) Tree
b) Positively affected
c) Negatively affected   Your answer: _____

Q.6. If you can control your performance arousal level so that you experience excitement at an appropriate level for your performing situation, you can:
a) Optimise and improve your level of performance
b) Achieve ideal results in your performing situation
c) Perform in The Zone
d) All of the above   Your answer: _____

Solution overleaf.

3. Why do we experience performance arousal anyway?

So now that you have a better idea of what performance arousal is, you might be wondering, "Why do we experience performance arousal anyway?" The purpose of this small chapter is to shed a little light on that very question.

The presence of others

In the late 19th century a psychologist by the name of N.D. Triplett observed for the first time that competitive cyclists rode faster when racing against one another than when racing alone. Triplett's findings triggered a considerable amount of research by many sports psychologists throughout the 20th century. Looking at all of this research, it turns out that we experience performance arousal when other people such as an audience, fans, onlookers, audition panel, or fellow performers are present. Research even shows that it is possible for us to experience performance arousal if we simply imagine that others are present.

Increase and decrease

Some of the studies that were carried out in sports psychology in the 20th century showed an improvement in performance level as a result of the presence of others. These studies proved that an appropriate level of excitement - positive performance arousal - can help us perform at a higher level.

Other 20th century studies by sports psychologists showed a decrease in performance level as a result of the presence of others. These studies suggest two different conclusions: The first is that being over-excited or not excited enough about a performance can create a negative effect on performance level. And secondly, nervousness or anxiety due to the presence of others can create a negative effect on performance.

Nature vs. nurture

Whether we experience performance arousal because of our genetic make up, or whether performance arousal is a learned, socially conditioned response is debateable. Studies supporting the nurture side of the debate suggest that we experience performance arousal because we've learned to associate the presence of an audience with performance evaluation or judgement.

Solution: Performance Arousal Multi-choice

Q.1. a)   Q.2. a)   Q.3. b)   Q.4. b)   Q.5. c)   Q.6. d)

Chapter 3

Believing that we are being evaluated or judged can create apprehension, as it can be linked to positive or negative outcomes for us as performers. This thereby increases the amount of performance arousal we experience.

On the opposite side of the debate, other studies concluded that the reason audiences create performance arousal in performers is because we are genetically designed to experience performance arousal. These studies discovered that the effects of performance arousal can be felt regardless of whether all other factors and processes that are commonly associated with the presence of others are eliminated. That is to say that we can experience performance arousal even though we're not in a competitive situation, told we are not being evaluated or judged, or are aware that the presence of an audience or spectators doesn't have any bearing on a potential reward or punishment. In other words, the nature argument says that performance arousal is a genetically designed response, and can be triggered simply by the presence of another person or persons – real, or imagined.

Whether we experience performance arousal due to 'nature', 'nurture', or a combination of both, the fact remains that performance arousal is a very real phenomenon, and something that can affect all who perform.

The Autonomous Nervous System

One of the most important systems of the human body is what is referred to as the Autonomous Nervous System. This is a type of control system in the body which is constantly operating throughout the course of our lives. It affects heart rate, digestion, respiration rate, perspiration, salivation, pupil diameter, and sexual excitement. The majority of the functions of the Autonomous Nervous System are just that, automatic and hence involuntary, however certain functions, such as breathing, can be controlled with the conscious mind.

Two branches

The Autonomous Nervous System can be talked about in terms of two main branches: The Parasympathetic Nervous System and the Sympathetic Nervous System.

The Parasympathetic Nervous System induces a calming and healing effect, enabling the body to rest, relax, and recover. The Sympathetic Nervous System creates activation and arousal, preparing the body for action, and is responsible for inducing the well-documented 'Fight or Flight' response.

Rather than acting against one another, the Parasympathetic and Sympathetic Nervous Systems are understood to be complementary, where the Sympathetic Nervous System can be likened to the accelerator pedal in a car, whilst the Parasympathetic Nervous System may be labelled as the brakes.

The 'Fight or Flight' response

It is commonly agreed upon that performance anxiety is triggered by a primitive urge that we all possess. This urge, or genetic programming, is commonly referred to as the 'Fight or Flight' response, and was partially responsible for the survival of our species through prehistoric times.

A little biology

38

In short, the 'Fight or Flight' response originates in an area of your brain called the hypothalamus. Whilst experiencing 'flight or flight', your hypothalamus tells your Sympathetic Nervous System to take control of your body's functions. When this happens, chemicals such as adrenaline and cortisol are released into your bloodstream, your rate of respiration increases, your heart rate becomes more rapid, your pupils dilate, your reflexes become more acute, and your perception of pain diminishes. Another way of putting it is that during 'Fight or Flight', you become both physically and psychologically prepared for 'the enemy', or other situations of perceived danger. Although useful in life-threatening situations where survival is paramount, the 'Fight or Flight' response in modern society and everyday situations is often experienced as a hindrance for performers and non-performers alike. It can even bring about phobias and other psychological problems.

A sabre-toothed audience?

In modern times, actual physical threats that require us to literally fight or run for our lives thankfully don't happen particularly frequently for the majority of us! However, perceived emotional threats such as performance evaluation, judgement, or the possibility of negative performance outcomes, happen to virtually everyone. Unfortunately however, these perceived emotional threats can elicit the same response in the brain as actual physical threats, even if the situations that cause these threats are vastly different. In other words, your brain may perceive mortal combat with sabre-toothed tigers to be equally as threatening as delivering a speech to an audience!

Relearning

As a performer (rather than a hunter-gatherer), if you can train your mind to consciously and sub-consciously understand that performance situations are non-threatening and indeed pleasurable, you can eliminate performance anxiety, obtain an ideal level of positive performance arousal for your performing situations, and ultimately achieve an optimal level of performance, regardless of your performance sphere. And the best news is that in practise, bringing your performance arousal level under control is not as complicated as it may seem!

4. How much positive performance arousal do you need?

As we've already seen, performance psychologists during the late 19th and 20th centuries made some important discoveries with regards to excitement and anxiety in performers. Although primarily concerned with sports-people, these discoveries can be directly applied to all performers, and have provided the necessary information for The Alternative Performance Equation to be derived, and the term 'performance arousal' to be defined. More detailed information about these discoveries can be found in Appendix 1: How The Zone diagrams were derived.

03
04

39

A closer look

In this chapter however we're going to take a closer look at the conclusions from Appendix 1, and find out exactly how much positive performance arousal (excitement) you need for various performing situations. To recap, what do you know about performance arousal so far? You've seen that:

- Performance arousal is a state of mind
- Performance arousal can take on two forms: anxiety and excitement
- Performance arousal can affect all performers
- Performance arousal is created by a response in your Autonomous Nervous System
- Performance arousal is experienced due to the presence of an audience (real or imagined)
- Performance arousal can affect both your body and mind
- Performance arousal can be mild or strong
- Performance arousal in its negative form (anxiety) can have a **negative** effect on your level of performance
- Performance arousal in its positive form (excitement) can have a **negative** effect on your level of performance if the amount of excitement you feel is **inappropriate** for your performing situation (for example, jumping up on tables and calling out to the crowd in a chess tournament)
- Performance arousal in its positive form (excitement) can have a **positive** effect on your level of performance if the amount of excitement you feel is **appropriate** for your performing situation (for example, jumping up on tables and calling out to the crowd in a professional wrestling match)

The Complete Performance Arousal Diagram, with all levels of performance arousal marked in:

40

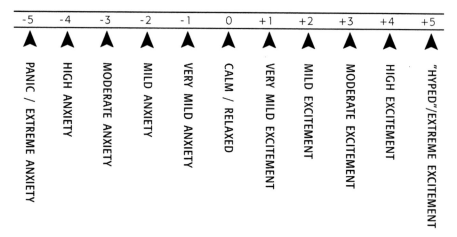

-5	-4	-3	-2	-1	0	+1	+2	+3	+4	+5
PANIC / EXTREME ANXIETY	HIGH ANXIETY	MODERATE ANXIETY	MILD ANXIETY	VERY MILD ANXIETY	CALM / RELAXED	VERY MILD EXCITEMENT	MILD EXCITEMENT	MODERATE EXCITEMENT	HIGH EXCITEMENT	"HYPED"/EXTREME EXCITEMENT

Using this diagram, you can see that a state of total calm and relaxation (possibly even meditation) is rated at 0. Extreme anxiety or panic is rated at -5. Extreme excitement or a feeling of being 'totally hyped' is given a +5 rating.

The negative numbers

As you've already seen in 'What do Professional Wrestlers and Chess Champions have in common?' the negative manifestation of performance arousal - anxiety - will always have a negative effect on your level of performance. The degree of the negative effect is directly proportional to the amount of anxiety experienced.

Not good for chess, professional wrestling, or any other performing situation!

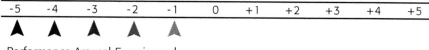

-5	-4	-3	-2	-1	0	+1	+2	+3	+4	+5

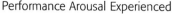

Performance Arousal Experienced

The following five examples show different levels of positive performance arousal (excitement) in various performing situations, and how this positive performance arousal can affect performance level. For the sake of visual clarity, the effects of anxiety and complete calm have been omitted from the diagrams.

Example situation 1: Public chess tournament

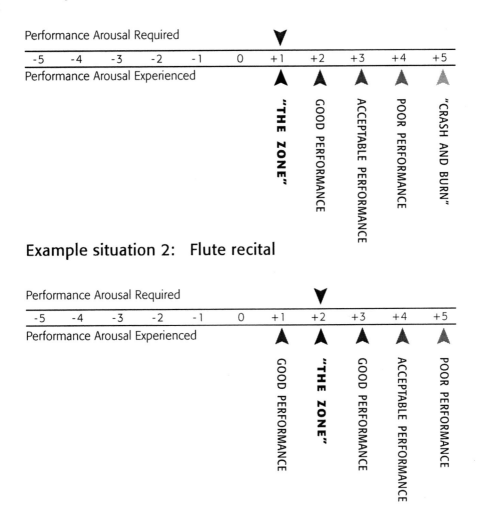

Example situation 2: Flute recital

Example situation 3: Public speaking engagement

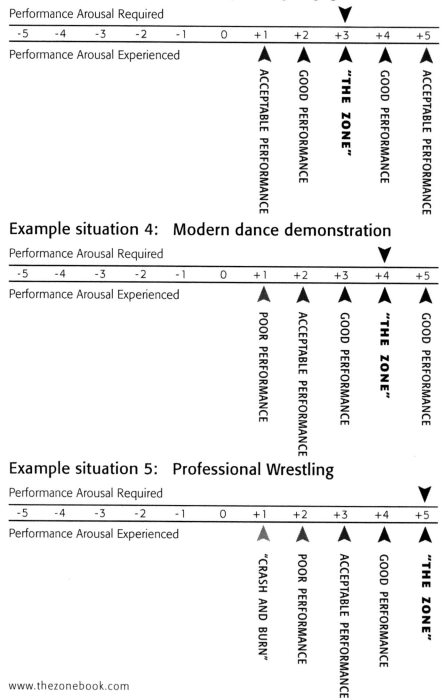

Example situation 4: Modern dance demonstration

Example situation 5: Professional Wrestling

These diagrams show that:

- If the amount of positive performance arousal (excitement) you experience is vastly different from the amount required for your performing situation, you can have a disastrous performance – you can 'Crash and Burn'.

- If the amount of positive performance arousal you experience is very different from the amount required for your performing situation, a negative result can occur (poor performance).

- If you experience performance arousal positively as excitement, but at a level that is mildly inappropriate for your performing situation, your resulting performance will probably be acceptable.

- If you experience performance arousal positively as excitement, and at a level that almost matches the amount needed for your performing situation, your resulting performance will be successful (good performance).

- And finally, to achieve the best performance level possible, the amount of positive performance arousal you experience must match the level of performance arousal required for your particular performing situation. When this happens, you can achieve optimal performance – you can perform in The Zone.

Being able to use specially designed tools and techniques to exert control over your performance arousal is the key to performing in The Zone.

You can learn to perform in The Zone!

At first, when learning to ride a bike or drive a car, you have to consciously learn certain physical and mental techniques. After time spent practising, your responses become automatic. That is to say that you eventually stop consciously thinking about the actions or thought processes you are carrying out, as you've already 'programmed' yourself to ride or drive successfully. And just as you can learn to ride a bike or drive a car, you can learn to obtain an ideal level of performance arousal in your performing situations. In other words, **you can learn to perform in The Zone!**

5. Why do you want to perform in The Zone?

In order to obtain a more appropriate level of performance arousal for your performing situations, or in fact make any genuine, positive change in your life, the following three questions can be of great help:

1. **What** do I want to achieve?
2. **Why** do I want to achieve this?
3. **How** do I achieve this?

What do I want to achieve?

If you don't know what it is that you are trying to achieve, you're probably not going to achieve it!

Why do I want to achieve this?

If you know what it is you want to achieve, but don't have any real reasons to achieve it, you will most likely lack the motivation required to achieve it.

How do I achieve this?

If you know both what you want to achieve and why you want to achieve it, but lack the skills, tools, techniques, or knowledge to achieve it, you will probably not achieve it.

The answers

So, because you are reading a copy of this book, I'm going to assume that your answer to the first question, "**What** do I want to achieve?" is something like:

"I want to obtain an ideal state of mind in my performing situations. I want to be able to control my performance arousal level. I want to perform in The Zone."

By knowing **why** you want to achieve this, you can create motivation and drive. Although the answer to the question "**Why** do you want to perform in The Zone?" may seem a little obvious at first, how much have you really thought about it? To create maximum drive and motivation, you must know **exactly why** you want to achieve your goal of performing in The Zone. Thinking about **exactly why** you want to achieve your goal of performing in The Zone is a good beginning. Verbalising your answer is a more effective option. However putting pen to paper (or fingers to the computer keyboard) is by far the most powerful solution.

An important motivation exercise

On the following pages you will find an exercise to complete right now to help you make clear to yourself exactly **what** it is you want to achieve, **why** you want to achieve it, and **how** you can achieve it.

You may choose to complete this exercise directly in this book, on a separate piece of paper, in a personal journal or diary, or on a computer. Complete this exercise before you read any more in this book! Be specific in your answers! This exercise may only take 5 minutes, but it could prove to be one of the most significant in your entire performing life!

5. Exercise: What, Why and How

Q: What do I want to achieve?

A: _____

_____

_____

_____

_____

Q: Why do I want to achieve this?

A: _____

_____

_____

_____

Q: What does this mean to me?

A: _____

_____

_____

_____

Q: How much do I want this?

A: _____

_____

_____

_____

Q: If at the end of my life I was to look back and realise that I hadn't made a 100% commitment to this, how would I feel?

A: _____

_____

_____

_____

_____

Q: How much enjoyment and satisfaction could I gain by doing this?

A: _____

_____

_____

_____

_____

Q: How much enjoyment and satisfaction could other people gain if I do this?

A: _____

_____

_____

_____

_____

Q: What positive effects could this have on my life?

A: _____

_____

_____

_____

_____

Q: What positive effects could this have on the lives of others?

A: _____

_____

_____

48   _____

_____

Q: How do I achieve this?

A: By studying and applying the techniques explained in Part Two of this book. By implementing The 12 Week Performance Success Programme outlined in Part Three. And if necessary, by studying and following up the complementary sources of help discussed in Part Four – Digging Deeper.

Once you've completed the exercise, read over the questions again, as well as your answers – preferably aloud. Were you specific? Did you complete all of the answers? You may like to share your answers with your partner, a close friend, colleague or teacher.

Now that you are completely clear about **what** you want to achieve, and **why** you want to achieve it, the last part is discovering **how** – a question that the rest of this book is dedicated to answering.

PART TWO
The Techniques

06
07
08
09
10
11
12
13
14
15
16
17
18
19
20
21
22
23
24
25
26
27
28
29
30
31
32
33

6. Introduction – Getting into The Zone

You may have heard the phrase, "you are what you eat." This is even now the title of a popular T.V. series in several countries. The age-old adage of "you are what you eat" is of course very true, and we'll discuss diet a little later on. However for now I'd like to change that timeless phrase a little and make the following statement:

You are what you think!

Your thought processes are responsible for everything about you – who you are, where you are, what you are doing, why you are doing it, and even how you are doing it. It is these very thought processes that are responsible for you holding a copy of this book! You are, quite simply, a result of your own thinking. How you perceive the world and indeed how you perceive yourself, as well as how you react and respond to these perceptions, is based entirely on how your mind operates.

You may like to think of your brain as a computer – one that is far more advanced than any piece of technology ever created by mankind. However as with all computers, regardless of how powerful, the phrase "junk in, junk out" still applies.

Perception

As a living, thinking, and feeling being, you have an immense intellectual and emotional capacity, whether you admit, or are fully aware of this fact or not. Given that your mind controls your perception of yourself and your perception of the world around you, it is logical then to say that if your mind perceives the proverbial glass as being 'half-empty', then that for you is a truth. Contrarily, if your mind perceives the same glass as being 'half-full', then that for you is a truth. Your particular perception of the glass will remain a 'truth' for you unless some external force, source of information, or realisation changes that perception.

It's more than just positive thinking

Of course there is a lot more to becoming a successful performer than simply positive thinking. As we've already seen, it takes a combination of cognitive (mental) attributes and physical skills, a resistance to external interference, and an ideal level of positive performance arousal – being in The Zone – to perform at your optimum level. As shown countless times in the history of performing and performers, and as The Alternative Performance Equation and other diagrams in Part One show, you simply cannot fulfil your true potential and achieve an optimal level of performance if you harbour negative thought processes, performance anxieties, doubt and the like, or if you become over-excited or apathetic in your performing situations. In other words as a performer, if your 'computer' is fed wrong information ("junk in") or **runs the wrong programs,** you will invariably get poor results ("junk out").

Chapter 6

Reprogramming

However, if you can alter, or 'reprogram' your state of mind and channel your energies correctly to suit your performing situation, you can optimise and improve your overall level of performance by achieving an ideal amount of positive performance arousal – you can in other words, with the right 'programming', learn to perform in The Zone.

The tools and techniques here in Part Two are designed to help you 'program' that fantastic 'computer' of yours so that it can work better for you in performing situations. These techniques provide your 'computer' (your mind) with quality input, allowing it to **run the right programs.** By using the techniques here in Part Two of *Performing in The Zone*, you can learn to be in the right state of mind for your performing situations, enabling you to unleash your true performing potential, and achieve an optimal level of performance, regardless of your performance sphere.

51

06

About Part Two

The many techniques in Part Two are presented in alphabetical order for ease of reference. There is a lot of information here, and many powerful tools, techniques, and exercises which you can experiment with, and adopt into your performing life.

To begin with, read through the various techniques provided here, experiment with them individually, and be sure to complete all of the exercises. Once you have some experience with the techniques, and when you feel ready, continue by following through with The 12 Week Performance Success Programme in Part Three. This programme has been designed to help you to enforce structure, provide motivation, and ultimately give you a massive boost in your journey towards performing in The Zone.

7. Add Value

What have you done today to add value to your own life?
What actions have you taken to add value to the lives of others?

An empowering question

"How does my performing add value to my own life as well as the lives of others?"
can be a very powerful question which can help you to remove anxiety and bring you
almost instantaneously closer to The Zone. For example, as an actor you may ask
yourself, "How is my acting tonight going to add value to my own life as well as the
lives of others?"

By concentrating on the second part of this question, the complete answer becomes
clear, and may be received in an instantaneous thought such as:

*"By performing tonight I will be touching the lives of many. The audience will have an experience
which they can feel emotionally connected to. They are here to receive this experience and I am
lucky enough to be able to give it to them. By me being here and simply doing my job, a job
which I enjoy, I am adding value to their lives. And in knowing that their lives have been
enriched, I also get satisfaction and pleasure, thereby adding value to my own life. It's a win-win
situation!"*

Your own personal answer or answers to the question "How does my performing add
value to my own life as well as the lives of others?" may of course take on shorter or
longer forms than the example given above.

Both parts of the question

Make sure though that you ask yourself both parts of the question. Unfortunately,
concentrating solely on the question "How can I add value to my own life", whilst
ignoring adding value to the lives of others, rarely has a positive outcome for
anyone.

Too often in human nature, to take value from other people's lives in order to enrich
our own is a trait which comes in many guises, and one which has the unfortunate
tendency to reoccur throughout the course of human history.

However, by asking the full question, "How can I add value to my own life as well as
the lives of others through my performing?" we break this negative cycle, and our
performing can have a small or even significant positive impact on the world around
us.

7. Exercise: How am I adding value?

Try to answer the following question in as much detail as possible:

How can my next performance add value to my own life, as well as the lives of others?

Read the question and your answer out loud.

Does your answer alter your perspective on the world around you?

How might your answer alter how you speak with and act towards other people?

_____

_____

_____

_____

_____

_____

_____

_____

How do you feel when answering this question on paper, and out loud?

_____

_____

_____

_____

_____

_____

_____

_____

_____

Imagine for a moment that if starting today and continuing for all time, every single person in our world asked themselves each and every day how they could add value to their own lives as well as others. A truly valuable concept.

8. Breathing

Breathing is a vital bodily function which for the most part is controlled by your Autonomous Nervous System, although it can also come under your conscious control. Breathing correctly is a pre-requisite for performing in The Zone, as the quality of your breathing has a significant effect on the level of performance arousal you experience, and whether it is manifested positively as excitement or negatively as anxiety.

Contradictions

Although there are many ideas already taught verbally and in print concerning the art of effective breathing, these sources and publications present a variety of opinions. At times these ideas and opinions appear seemingly contradictory. This may be due to several reasons.

The first reason could be incorrect sensory awareness. That is, what many teachers and performers (especially singers and players of wind instruments) think they do when breathing is often quite different from what they actually do. In addition, when the act of breathing is described, the language used often includes incorrect terminology. And even when correct terminology is used, these words can be easily misinterpreted. Adding to this confusion, the vast majority of us can be described as poor, or incorrect breathers, therefore what is considered to be 'normal', is not always the most natural or correct means of breathing. And finally, even if a performer is breathing naturally or 'correctly', it can be difficult for a student, onlooker or fellow performer to observe this from the outside.

A natural approach

Given the reasons above, I've purposely avoided stating "breathe in this way or that" to achieve optimum performance arousal and enter The Zone. Rather, the majority of the techniques demonstrated in this section, Part Two: The Techniques, are designed to optimise your breathing by getting you to focus on what you would like to achieve, the mind state you need to be in, a particular thought or idea, or the task at hand, rather than the act of breathing itself. This in turn automatically affects your quality of breathing – increasing the rate and activation for situations requiring high levels of performance arousal, and slowing the rate and relaxing the breath for situations requiring lower levels of performance arousal.

So, by focussing on a specific technique from this part of *Performing in The Zone*, you simply let go, allowing your Autonomous Nervous System do its job. In this way, you avoid the need to exert conscious control over the breath.

9. Cue Cards

It may be useful for you to assign a number from the performance arousal continuum to the specific level of performance arousal you wish to obtain. For example, if you are a dancer about to give a high-energy show, you might imagine that +4 on the performance arousal scale is ideal (high energy, high excitement, strong positive feeling), whereas if you are a corporate executive about to give a speech to a board of directors, you may prefer +1 (positive, assured, very mild excitement).

Referring to Cue Cards

For various reasons, at times before performances you may find it difficult remembering which level of performance arousal is optimal for your performing situation, which techniques from *Performing in The Zone* you need to implement, and which Pre-Performance Rituals (see Chapter 25) you need to carry out. A quick, easy, and effective way to remind yourself is by creating and referring to Cue Cards.

Referring to Cue Cards should be possible for the majority of performers immediately prior to performance events. In the case of some performers, such as musicians reading music from music stands, or public speakers referring to notes, Cue Cards can even be used during a performance, without the knowledge of the audience. If you are a musician or public speaker, instead of making actual cards to refer to, you may decide to simply write down key words such as those given in the example below on your music or in your notes if appropriate.

Key words written on Cue Cards should be very simple reminders or triggers. A Cue Card may look something like this:

Go Peripheral
+3
funky • fun • free

In this example, the performer is about to audition for a popular televised singing contest. The level of performance arousal they wish to achieve is a strong +3, as the chosen audition song has a moderate tempo and a heavy 'groove'. The Cue Card is kept handy at all times before the performance, and simply slipped into their pocket immediately before entering the audition room.

Chapter 9

The three lines of information

On the Cue Card, there are three lines of information. The first, Go Peripheral, refers to a technique which can be used to exert direct control over performance arousal level. This technique is discussed in detail in Chapter 15. The second line, '+3', is a reminder of where the auditionee wants to be on the performance arousal continuum: positive, with a moderately high level of energy, perfect for the audition song. The third line is a reminder to execute a specific Mantra, discussed in Chapter 25. In this case the auditionee has decided to use F3 to achieve a 'funky, fun, and free' feeling. Cue Cards and the words written on them, such as in the above example, can act as powerful triggers to bring you closer to The Zone in your performing situations.

9. Exercise: Cue…your Cue Card!

For your next three performances, regardless of how significant or insignificant they may seem, create and refer to Cue Cards. Remember to include the level of performance arousal you would like to achieve, as well as reminders of any techniques or Pre-Performance Rituals you would like to use.

Upon completion of your performances, note the effects of your Cue Cards in the spaces below.

Performance 1:

_____

_____

_____

_____

Performance 2:

_____

_____

_____

_____

Performance 3:

_____

_____

_____

_____

You may also like to ask yourself the following: How can I improve my Cue Cards to help me to an even greater extent for my next performance?

_____

_____

_____

_____

10. Excessive Talk, and Silence

The performers who consistently achieve the best results by being in The Zone rarely feel the need to tell everybody else how great they are, how good they look, how impressive their last show, event, or competition was and so on. Instead, they let their performances do the talking. Likewise, if successful performers for whatever reason have a bad day, they rarely advertise this fact to those around them. However contrarily to this, it is common to see less successful performers 'beating themselves up' by telling people how much better they could have or should have done, or 'putting themselves on pedestals' by telling everyone exactly how great they are – often at the same time informing of all of the faults they find in others.

Ancient wisdom
The following ancient Chinese proverb coined by Lao Tzu eloquently sums up excessive talk: *"Those who know do not speak. Those who speak do not know."*
This quote is so important in your life as a performer. Why?

The ego
Because by verbalising how great you are and how awful others are, or how awful you are and how great everyone else is, the ego – that spoiled brat part of your psyche – is allowed to run wild. However by silencing excessive verbalisation, you can take the first step to silencing the ego.

Why is silencing the ego so important?
Because the ego is what is responsible for thought processes such as "What will they think of me if such and such happens? What if I fail? What if I can't do it? What if it doesn't work?", as well as all of those other negatively charged "What if?" statements. Your ego wants to do anything it can to protect itself, feel safe, survive, and feel 100% at the centre of the world. Therefore it can create thought patterns which can lead to anxieties, as well as self-centredness and a false sense of self-importance. These negative thought patterns or 'programs' are not conducive to successful performing or a balanced life!

How can we break the cycle of excessive talk and silence the ego?
There are several ways to do this. One of the most powerful tools we have to silence the ego is to examine the concept of **Living in The Now,** discussed in Chapter 20. Another approach is to employ the **Add Value** technique mentioned in Chapter 7. A third approach to silencing the ego as well as excessive talk is to take a temporary vow of silence and simply stop talking!

Silent retreats

Many countries have specific organisations offering silent retreats. The format of these silent retreats can vary, however the basic idea is that you, along with a group, move to a location, often in the countryside, and live there for a period of a few days, a week, or longer. Some silent retreats include a pen and paper for their guests, whereas others encourage absolutely no form of communication whatsoever for their guests for the entire duration of their stay. Counsellors and coaches may be on hand to offer help and support if necessary.

The results experienced by ordinary people participating in silent retreats are often very powerful, with many expressing afterwards that their retreat was a "life-changing" or "mind-blowing" experience. Such an experience could also be valuable for you in your search for an ideal state of mind for your performing situations.

As an alternative to a silent retreat, you may choose to set aside a certain period of silent time each day, possibly to be included as a part of your **My Time** (see Chapter 21). By inducing silence, you can calm your mind, silence your ego, and create a stable platform for entering The Zone.

10. Exercise: Give it a rest!

Set aside 15 minutes each day for silence, in a sitting, standing, kneeling, or horizontal posture. During these 15 minutes you are to do nothing. Simply remain quiet, conscious, and aware. Observe your surroundings, but don't comment, analyse, or pass judgement on them. Enjoy this state of silence, not uttering a single word, or communicating in any way for a full 15 minutes. The silent state is a passive state, and therefore reading, writing emails, or watching T.V. does not count as a silent, passive state.

61

In your chosen posture, enjoy the freedom, the release, and the rest that silence brings. You may experience your ego making its presence felt by telling you that this is 'a waste of time' for example. If these thoughts come, simply let them float away. Spending 15 minutes in a silent state each morning can help to put you in a calm and grounded state for the rest of the day. A truly valuable investment of time!

10

At first it may seem difficult to allow yourself a full 15 minutes of silence each day. However the more you do it, the easier it gets! As a way to build up, you may like to begin by spending just 1 minute in a silent state each day. Then build up to 2 minutes, 5 minutes, 10 minutes, and then 15 minutes. Once you become accustomed to 15 minutes of silence, you may even experiment by spending longer periods of time in a silent state.

Experiment with and enjoy the benefits of the peace and tranquillity that silence brings. In time, you too will see exactly why "Silence is golden", and how it can help you towards performing in The Zone.

11. E=mc²

Albert Einstein's famous theory of relativity: $E=mc^2$. That is, energy is equal to mass, multiplied by the speed of light squared. In other words, Einstein means that energy and mass are interchangeable; the amount of energy in a closed system remains constant because energy cannot be created or destroyed; and that trapped energy is always manifested as mass. This concept occurs in everyday situations and is not as complicated as it may seem.

A little physics

For example: A candle burns. Its mass is converted to heat energy as it is burning. When the mass is gone, the flame is extinguished. Where did the candle go? Did it simply vanish into thin air? More or less, yes. The candle was converted to heat energy, which was then dispersed into the air. The candle became a part of its surroundings if you will – mass became energy.

So how does this relate to you and performing?

Energy is everything. That means that you too are made up of energy. This energy is manifested as your mass. You take in energy primarily through the food and drink that you consume. You also receive energy from fresh air in the form of oxygen, negative ions, or as Eastern philosophies describe it, Qi. Further studies into Qi Gong show that we can even harness energy from other sources.

What you need to do is learn how to focus and control your energy. You already know how to make a candle disappear! Just strike a match, wait a few hours, and the 'magic trick' is completed.

Energy and performance arousal

The state of our energy can be altered by our interactions with other people and the world around us. Energy can pass through us, such as in the form of electric shocks, or it can be stored in us, such as when emotional baggage and unresolved negative experiences take on chronic physiological symptoms, well documented in both Eastern and Western science.

Performance arousal therefore is simply energy in motion, taking on particular forms, as a result of our interactions with the physical world and direction from our minds. This description may seem too brief and all too existential to fully comprehend here. However, a more in-depth discussion and explanation of ourselves as beings of energy is unfortunately far beyond the scope of this book. For further enlightenment in this subject, several of the books listed in the section Bibliography and Suggested Further Reading may be of interest.

But for now, it's back to you, and how to get to The Zone.
If you are experiencing a -5 on the performance arousal scale, you are panicking, or using colloquial language 'freaking out'. The high level of energy you require to experience extreme anxiety comes from within you and is unleashed as the 'Fight or Flight' response. If you indeed decide to fight or flee, the stored energy will be converted into kinetic and heat energy – in other words, your body in motion. However if you don't fight or flee, this negatively manifested energy, this -5, can stay with you and cause all sorts of physical and psychological symptoms – quivering hands, sweaty palms, hyperventilation and so on. Again using colloquial terms, if you are 'totally psyched up' and at the other end of the scale at a +5, this high level of energy is also coming from the same place – within you. The trigger for this energy to be set in motion may come from an external source – the audience for example, or an internal source – thinking about the outcome of the performance. However, what is important to realise is that the energy required to move you from a calm state to a highly anxious or highly excited state, comes from inside of you.

The E=mc² technique
Explained below, the direct approach of the $E=mc^2$ technique for controlling performance arousal is not for all performers, but may work for you. The best way to find out if this technique will work for you is to experiment with it in your practise, training, or rehearsal sessions. When you feel comfortable enough with the $E=mc^2$ technique, you can apply it to real life performing situations.

How it works - an example
To adopt the $E=mc^2$ technique, you must firstly be able to assess your current position on the performance arousal scale immediately prior to your performance event. You also have to know how much positive performance arousal you need in order to achieve optimal performance. For example, you are minutes before making an important presentation, and feeling uneasy. You assess your performance arousal level at a -3 on the scale – moderately worried, and anxious about the outcome. You may like to use a Cue Card to remind you to adopt the $E=mc^2$ technique, as it can be difficult to think clearly when at the extreme ends of the performance arousal continuum.

You are about to walk into the performance environment, and know that you need to be at a +2 on the performance arousal scale to be most effective – mild excitement, and with a positive feeling. A +2 on the performance arousal scale will help you to perform in The Zone in this particular performing situation.

11a. Exercise: Practising the E=mc² technique

Close your eyes.

Imagine seeing the performance arousal scale in front of you.
You see a marker at -3 on the scale. Breathe in gently.

In your mind, gradually slide the marker sitting at -3 to -2 whilst breathing out imagined negative energy. You may like to experiment by imagining negative energy as a dark grey cloud. Then breathe in imagined positive energy. You may like to experiment by imagining positive energy as warm, golden-coloured light.

Now gradually slide the marker in your mind from -2 to -1, again breathing out imagined negative energy. Breathe in imagined positive energy.

Gradually slide the marker in your mind from -1 to 0, again breathing out imagined negative energy. Breathe in imagined positive energy.

Gradually slide the marker in your mind from 0 to +1, again breathing out imagined negative energy. Breathe in imagined positive energy.

Gradually slide the marker in your mind from +1 to +2, again breathing out imagined negative energy. Breathe in imagined positive energy.

You might imagine this process as in the figure below.

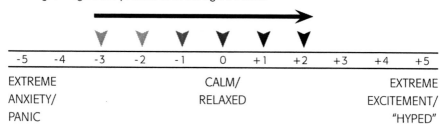

| -5 | -4 | -3 | -2 | -1 | 0 | +1 | +2 | +3 | +4 | +5 |

EXTREME	CALM/	EXTREME
ANXIETY/	RELAXED	EXCITEMENT/
PANIC		"HYPED"

Go through this exercise, and then re-assess where you are on the performance arousal scale. If you aren't yet at your ideal level of performance arousal, repeat the exercise, remembering to exhale imagined negative energy with each movement of the marker, and inhale positive energy in the pauses between movements. Complete this exercise slowly. If you are standing, make sure your posture is erect and relaxed. You can even adopt the Qi Gong posture as described in Chapter 26.

11b. Exercise: Applying the E=mc² technique

In your next practise or performing situation, experiment with the E=mc² technique.

Assess where you are on the performance arousal scale before you begin, and make sure you know how much positive performance arousal you need to have to be in The Zone for your particular performing situation. Close your eyes. Gradually move the marker to where it needs to be, breathing in and out with each movement. Record your results below:

Rehearsal / performing situation:

_____

_____

My performance arousal level before using the E=mc² technique:

_____

_____

My ideal performance arousal level for the performing situation:

_____

_____

My performance arousal level after using the E=mc² technique:

_____

_____

How I can improve the E=mc² technique for my own performing situations:

_____

_____

With practise, the E=mc² technique can be a powerful tool for locking onto an ideal level of performance arousal and helping you to perform in The Zone. And what is particularly interesting is that Einstein's equation is the basis for all of the techniques in this book, as indeed, "energy is everything."

12. Feign Confidence

Similar to Role Play described in Chapter 27, one very simple technique that you can employ at any time to get you performing in The Zone is the technique of Feigning Confidence. With this technique, you simply forget about any uncertainty that may exist inside of you, and just pretend to be confident.

"Well I'm not confident!" you might say.

That's okay! Just try the next exercise...

12a. Exercise: If I was confident...

Ask yourself the following:

1. How would I stand if I was confident?
    Stand confidently for a few minutes **right now!**

2. How would I walk if I was confident?
    Walk confidently for a few minutes **right now!**

3. How would I move my body if I was confident?
    Move your body confidently for a few minutes **right now!**

4. How would my voice sound if I was confident?
    Speak confidently for a few minutes **right now!**
    (say anything – read the text from this page aloud for example)

5. How would I expect other people to react to me if I was confident?
    Think about this for a few minutes **right now!**

6. How would it feel being confident?
    Think about this for a few minutes **right now!**

Asking yourself these questions and going through the different parts of this exercise can help to focus your mind on how great it would be if you were confident. This starts to create a positive thought process. The knock-on effect is that if you truly focus on answering these questions, you can actually end up being confident!

In addition, you might like to try adopting the following 5 Tips for Feigning Confidence. You may be amazed at the power of Feigning Confidence, and how it can affect not only your performing life, but your social interactions as well.

Chapter 12

5 Tips for Feigning Confidence

Tip 1: Posture
Sit or stand with an erect posture – relaxed, with a straight spine, your chest up and shoulders back. Your head should be directly on top of your spine, effortlessly balanced on a relaxed neck, and not slumped forwards or to one side of you.

Tip 2: Eye contact
Briefly make eye contact with other people or members of your audience if appropriate. You don't need to try to stare them down, simply show them that you are an open person, willing to communicate.

Tip 3: Smile
If appropriate in your performance situation, a smile can go a long way to making your audience feel at ease. Their comfort level is then automatically directed back to you, and can give you a sense of security.

Tip 4: Be playful
Being a little light-hearted or playful in non-performing situations can have the knock-on effect of making any performance situation seem less of a 'big deal', helping your confidence.

Tip 5: Remember
Remember who you are and where you come from. Be proud of your achievements thus far. Celebrate your uniqueness.
In addition, remember that you have a worth. You have a value, and in performing you are adding value not only to your own life, but the lives of others.

You can begin practising Feigning Confidence by entering any situation where there are people present that you have previously not met before – social gatherings, cafés, and shops are ideal locations.

Respectful confidence

An important note here. There is a significant difference between confidence and arrogance. Be respectful and charming – that's confidence! By demonstrating respectful confidence, feigned or not, you communicate to others that you have a high personal self-esteem, self-worth, and value. Other people, whether they be audience members or locals at a bar or nightclub, automatically sense this. Knowing that you are viewed as having a high value can reinforce your confidence. In this way, it doesn't matter if your original confidence was feigned or not, as within a short space of time, you will be experiencing real confidence!

Whether you are entering a performance or non-performance situation, remember that if you are not feeling confident, all you have to do to achieve confidence is pretend! You can even use a Cue Card to remind yourself of this powerful technique.

12b. Exercise: Feigning it

The next time you are at a public gathering or in a performing situation, experiment with Feigning Confidence. You may like to think the words "Feign Confidence", ask yourself the questions from the 'If I was confident…' exercise, or you may like to concentrate on one or several of the '5 Tips for Feigning Confidence' given above. Note how Feigning Confidence can induce real confidence.

What I could do to Feign Confidence in a performing or social situation:

_____

_____

_____

_____

How Feigning Confidence helped me in a performing or social situation:

_____

_____

_____

_____

_____

13. Free Writing

When we sleep, we dream – whether we remember those dreams when we wake up or not. Dreaming is a way for our 'super-computer', our brain, to file, categorise, understand, and process the events of the current day, the past, and even make the foundations of our future plans, using information taken in through all five senses, consciously and subconsciously. Free Writing is a continuation of this nocturnal process – a sort of 'dreaming while being awake'. The advantage of Free Writing however is that if you choose to, you can later go back and see exactly what it was that your brain was processing. In some cases Free Writing can expose certain emotional blocks or thought patterns which may have been impeding your progress towards The Zone. Once these thought patterns or blocks have been made tangible, it is often easier to deal with them and move on.

Lightening the mental load

Free Writing can spawn great ideas, or simply lighten the mental load by gently bringing thoughts forward from the innermost murmurings of your brain, and putting them on paper. Again using technology as a metaphor, you might say that Free Writing allows your brain – your 'super-computer' – to free up its RAM by using virtual memory, or a 'swap file'.

Topics

When Free Writing, no topics are taboo, nor do you need to feel pressed to write about any subject in particular. You may simply write your plan for the day, shopping list, express your reaction to a conversation you had previously, become profound and philosophical, or even express your thoughts about the Free Writing itself. If you get stuck, some concrete topics you may like to explore could be your thoughts about:

- a previous or up-coming performance
- a list of the positive emotions you've felt over the past days (happy, excited etc) and what made you feel those emotions
- a list of the negative emotions you've felt over the past days (sad, worried, anxious etc) and ways you might alleviate these emotions
- positive internal and external qualities that you have which make you unique
- the things you are truly grateful for in your life

The point here is to write something. Try to keep your pen moving for the duration of your Free Writing session. You may perhaps even begin with just single words, and then gradually progress to phrases and more complex entries.

Meaning

Sooner or later, amongst the words you will find meaning in your writing. The entire process lightens the load of the mind by getting your thoughts and feelings out on paper – or on the computer screen – whichever works best for you. Spelling, grammar, punctuation and form are irrelevant here. You may wish to keep the words, phrases, stories, and ideas expressed during your Free Writing private. Alternatively, you may choose to share certain Free Writing entries with the people closest to you. Whether or not you choose to share your Free Writing is completely up to you.

Keeping a Free Writing journal

For archiving purposes, a hard-backed blank journal is ideal (loose pages easily get damaged or lost). Alternatively, you can simply create a new file on your computer called "Free Writing." You may even choose to start an anonymous 'blog' on the internet for your Free Writing.

Free Writing and emotional release

It is not unusual to experience laughter, sadness, rage, sorrow, or other powerful emotions during the Free Writing process. These symptoms are natural and should neither be encouraged nor repressed. They are simply a healthy sign that the process of emotional release is taking place. Simply experience whatever needs be expressed, and as you do so, let the emotions go. Although writing while travelling to a school or workplace may give results for some, the emotional release that Free Writing can occasionally bring about may be mildly distressing to those in your close vicinity. Therefore, it is best to carry out the technique of Free Writing in private – either indoors at your own home, or at an outdoor location where you know you won't be disturbed.

The results of Free Writing can vary greatly between people. Some may never experience dramatic emotional release, whilst others may experience this frequently.

How to get started

To start your Free Writing, put a date at the beginning of each entry on your chosen form of media – paper or digital. You may choose to start by writing for 15 minutes each morning for a week, perhaps as you eat breakfast. You can then gradually increase your Free Writing time up to 20 or even 30 minutes or more as you wish. Just as when you sleep, it is crucial that you are not disturbed by others when you write. After a period of several weeks, you may wish to review your entries. Have you discovered something you didn't previously know about yourself? Was there a great idea for your next performance in there somewhere? Did you find a solution to a problem? Did you experience some form of emotional release? Perhaps you came up with your own technique or techniques to help improve your level of performance and get you closer to The Zone?

Summary

Remember, in Free Writing there are no rules, no absolutes, no right or wrong. Here, you are completely free. Due to the absence of rules, the process of expressing yourself with Free Writing can be extremely liberating. It can help unlock old emotional barriers, allowing easier access to your full potential and hence easier access to The Zone.

71

13

14. Get a Coach

By going it alone, the techniques and exercises in this book can help you to take control of your performance arousal level, bringing about some fantastic results by getting you closer to The Zone in your field of performance. In addition, having a personal coach to encourage, support, and motivate you along your path to The Zone can provide a powerful additional source of help.

Different roles

Many successful sports teams and individual sports people employ the service of dedicated, knowledgeable, and experienced coaches. A coach may fill several roles – expert, trainer, motivator, mentor or even therapist. Different coaches employ different strategies but the end goal is always the same – to help bring out the best in their athletes, or rather, to help the athletes to bring out the best in themselves.

Different guises

Coaches can also come in many other guises. For example, your partner, children, friends, family, or colleagues may be your best sources of motivation, encouragement, and support – the best coaches – for you in your current situation. In addition, specialist lifestyle coaches, motivational speakers, and therapists with experience in specific mental training strategies such as Neuro-Linguistic Programming (NLP), can be of immense benefit.

Being coached

If you already have a coach, show them a copy of this book. Alternatively, you could direct your coach to www.thezonebook.com where they can pick up their own copy. Ask your coach to read through *Performing in The Zone*, and get them to see if there are exercises, techniques, or other parts of this book that they could help you with.

If you don't already have a coach, regardless of your ability and experience, and regardless of how your level of performance arousal is manifested, you may benefit from having a private coach or mentor.

You can seek out the help of a professional coach in your area, enlist the alternative approach of having friends, family or colleagues to provide support, inspiration, and motivation for you, or request private coaching through www.thezonebook.com

A personal choice

You may feel that your personal journey to The Zone is a process that you prefer not to share with others, and therefore may decide at this point in time that private coaching is not for you. This is of course totally okay! Quite simply, if it works for you, do it!

Chapter 14

The exercises and techniques provided in this book are designed so that you can carry them out successfully and effectively without the aid of others. These exercises and techniques, combined with The 12 Week Performance Success Programme in Part Three and the complementary sources of help outlined in Part Four: Digging Deeper, may very well be all that is required for you to learn how to control your performance arousal level, enter The Zone, and achieve an optimum level of performance. Whether you currently have a coach, decide to enlist the help of a coach, or whether you decide to pursue your journey to The Zone unassisted, be sure to take the time you need to read, understand, and implement the exercises, techniques, and The 12 Week Performance Success Programme given in this book.

With practise and patience, with or without the aid of a coach, you can make it to The Zone!

14

14. Exercise: Find a coach

Find five possible coaches that could help you to perform in The Zone:

1.

_____

2.

_____

3.

_____

4.

_____

5.

_____

15. Going Peripheral

Have you ever seen one of those nature documentaries, and noticed what happens when an animal gets startled? Its eyes widen, and its fur sticks up on end. It freezes for a second, and then disappears into the night. Converted into human terms, you might say that in a stressful situation your eyes widen, your palms start to sweat, you freeze for a second, you feel like you want to run off into the night, but you know that you can't and instead have to stay in that situation until it's over.

75

Eyes and vision

Your eyes, or rather, the external and internal muscles controlling their movement and appearance, can display a vast range of emotions, easily interpreted by other people as well as animals. You know if someone is genuinely happy not by how wide their smile is, but if their eyes are 'smiling' too.

Similarly you can see if someone is experiencing an extreme level of performance arousal, positive or negative, by looking at their eyes and the muscles around them. How your eyes function and indeed what you see and how you interpret what you see is different when experiencing a high level of performance arousal (+5 or -5), compared to when performance arousal is low (+1 or -1), or non-existent (0). This ocular reflex is controlled by the Autonomous Nervous System, mentioned earlier, but can also come under your conscious control.

14
15

Tunnel vision

When your Sympathetic Nervous System is highly active, for example when experiencing the 'Fight or Flight' response, you can experience a sort of tunnel vision. In this state, your eyes make swift, jerky movements as a natural way of looking for 'the enemy'. When this happens, objects directly in front of you are perceived as more prominent, whilst objects to the side of your main focus, and out in the periphery are often not registered.

Applying the brakes

If you are in a situation where you need to reduce the amount of performance arousal you are experiencing, or counter the effects of anxiety, taking conscious control over your eyes can help. By using the technique of Going Peripheral, you can lessen the activation of your Sympathetic Nervous System (the accelerator pedal), and trigger your Parasympathetic Nervous System (the brakes), creating a calming effect on your body and mind.

To Go Peripheral, follow these steps:

1. Look straight ahead.
2. Relax your eyes – or even close them slightly.
3. Focus on objects or the walls at the extreme left and right of you, without moving your eyes.
4. Maintain this attention to your peripheral vision for as long as you feel necessary, but at least 30 seconds.

Going Peripheral can aid you in restoring control to your body and mind if you feel over-excited, nervous or anxious in performing and non-performing situations alike.

This technique has its strongest effect when sitting, reclining, or incorporating the standing posture explained in the first 4 steps of the Qi Gong Basic Horse-stance Standing Meditation exercise in Chapter 26.

15. Exercise: The Going Peripheral Experiment

Try Going Peripheral now using the steps given above.

What effects does Going Peripheral have on you?

_____

_____

_____

_____

_____

You may notice that your breathing slows down, and that you begin to relax muscles in the rest of your body.

If you can't 'Go Peripheral' immediately, don't worry. It may be a new technique for you which might require a little practise. In a short time though, Going Peripheral will be an effective technique that you will be able to execute at any time in any situation to alleviate anxiety, and reduce your overall level of performance arousal. If your performance situations require physical and mental calm, Going Peripheral can help you to get closer to The Zone.

16. Keep a Balanced Life
– You are more than what you do!

Becoming a successful performer, or in fact successful at anything, requires a great deal of devotion, regardless of natural talent. A large amount of your time, energy and focus must be spent on your field of performance – these are of course pre-requisites for your success. However by concentrating only on your performance arena, that is to say one-sidedness or tunnel vision, you may inadvertently create a very real series of problems for yourself.

A precarious position

As specialist performers, we have specific abilities that are on a higher level than non-specialist performers. For example we may be physically stronger in certain muscle groups, more flexible, have greater coordination, faster reflexes, or have a more complete knowledge of tactics and techniques within our own specialty field of performance. However as a performer, if you are only as much as what you do and nothing more, you may be putting yourself in a very precarious position, possibly without even knowing it. Such a position can show itself if an event occurs which prevents you from performing at the level you are accustomed to. Or, worse still, if this event prevents you from performing altogether. Logic says that if you are only as much as what you do – a performer in a specific genre – a debilitating event in your performance life would be responsible for you simply not being! However this is of course not the case.

An example

Let's say you are a dancer and sustain an injury which prevents you from having the same physical capacity to dance. If you were only a dancer and nothing else, logic says that you in fact cease then to exist. But you don't cease to exist in reality! You are very much still you, just unable to perform in this one field as you once could in the past. So, what could you do? There are of course many options available if you are open enough to receive them. You may choose to pursue old interests outside of your performance arena, or foster completely new interests. For example you may have always wondered what it would be like to become a choreographer, production manager, stage manager, or lighting designer. There are many possibilities.

Other options

This same situation of an unexpected end to a career can occur in sports people, musicians, actors, or in fact any performer in any field. Catastrophe is an event that we never expect, and certainly never wish for. You should of course plan for and expect the best – total success – but be open to other possibilities if and when you need them.

Chapter 16

Short careers

Some performers in certain fields reach an age where they are no longer capable of performing to a level which is satisfying to them, or those around them. Competitive gymnasts, dancers, and many elite athletes for example often have a relatively short performing life, and must inevitably seek new challenges when their performing careers come to a conclusion. Often the challenge and fulfilment of teaching or coaching is a natural next step for many.

79

An understanding

By understanding that you are more than what you do, worrying thoughts such as "What happens if I get an injury which prevents me from performing? What will I do then?" lose their potency. Knowing that you have answers to these questions can therefore be very comforting and liberating, eliminating a possible cause of negative performance arousal, thereby making The Zone more easily obtainable.

Other avenues

The message here is that you are more than what you do – even if you aren't exactly certain what that is right now. Opening your mind to new opportunities and interests will help you discover these other parts of your persona.

16

It is important to realise that other avenues to explore need not take anything away from your chosen field of expertise. In fact, new interests may even prove to be of significant benefit to you by broadening your knowledge and understanding of various aspects of your chosen field of performance, as well as increasing your own range of skills and abilities. For example, teaching in your field of performance, and coaching others, are some of the most powerful ways of discovering more about yourself and your performance sphere. At the same time as helping someone else, you inevitably help yourself in a myriad of ways.

You may wish to try the following exercise to discover some other interests which can be of benefit to your performing life, and yourself as a whole.

16. Exercise: The well-rounded performer

1. My chosen field of performance:

_____

_____

_____

2. One interest which I can explore which could compliment my chosen field of performance:

_____

_____

_____

3. One interest which I can explore which could provide me with a refreshing break from my field of performance, if and when needed:

_____

_____

_____

4. One interest which I could pursue, if I was unable to continue performing in my chosen field for whatever reason:

_____

_____

_____

17. Keep a Performance Journal

If not documented, amazing performances and achievements can easily be forgotten. Although important, a CV, biography, or brief presentation about yourself is not suitable as a means for fully documenting your performance history. Therefore, keeping a performance journal can be an invaluable reminder for all of the amazing performances and achievements you have produced throughout your performing life. In addition, it can serve as a historical document which others may also gain knowledge and enjoyment from referring to.

A gentle reminder

If your confidence is ever shaken for whatever reason, a performance journal can help remind you that you have many successful performances behind you, which no person, criticism or event can ever take away from you. By using a performance journal, your performances become immortalised. These memories, much like a photo album, can be shared with others and even passed on to future generations as you wish.

Format

A performance journal can be a combination of a scrapbook and diary. You might like to purchase a hard-backed book with blank pages, in A4 or A5 format, to use as your performance journal. By using a dedicated book, you can save reviews, photographs, newspaper articles, and even record audience responses, as well as your own thoughts about each performance. Using a computer for your performance journal is also a possibility.

Keeping a performance journal is also an integral part of the technique Practising Performing – 5 Steps to Mastery, which we'll come to in Chapter 24.

On the next page you'll find a template which you may photocopy freely and use for your performance journal.

17. Performance Journal

Day/Date/Time   _____

Location   _____

Event/performance name   _____

Performance arousal level(s) required   _____

Performance arousal level(s) experienced   _____

Techniques utilised

_____

_____

_____

Noted positive effects

_____

_____

_____

_____

What did I do well?

_____

_____

_____

What can I improve?

_____

_____

_____

Notes

_____

_____

_____

18. Laughing Yoga

Disclaimer: The information given below is in no way intended to replace specialist medical advice provided by a health professional. Should you suspect that you have a health problem you should visit a health professional immediately.

A rather strange practise to the uninitiated, Laughing Yoga or Hasya Yoga as it is referred to in India, is quickly gaining popularity here in the West, especially in the high-stress environments of larger cities. The practise of Laughing Yoga was made popular by Dr. Madan Kataria, a physician from Mumbai, India.

83

Health benefits
A mere 20 to 30 minutes each day of this Indian health regime has been proven to elicit the following benefits: an increase of oxygen levels in the blood; a reduction in stress; a boost to the immune system; relief of depression, anxiety, and anger; regulation of blood pressure; and even a significant reduction in cold and flu symptoms. These benefits can have a direct positive impact on us as performers, reducing negative performance arousal, and helping to bring us closer to performing in The Zone.

How to practise
The best way to practise Laughing Yoga is with others. With over 6000 clubs in 60 countries, (at the time of writing), there may very well be a Laughing Yoga group in your city. Often these classes are free, and take place in public locations. The easiest way to locate a group near you is to search Dr. Kataria's Laughing Yoga website at www.laughteryoga.org

17
18

If you can't find a group to join, you can form your own group and begin experimenting with Laughing Yoga with others. Alternatively, you may try it by yourself. Note however that Laughing Yoga has been known to raise a few eyebrows so you may wish to practise in private if trying this technique by yourself!

18. Exercise: Laughing Yoga

The best way to begin practising Laughing Yoga is to induce a fake or forced laughter. The fantastic thing about this is that the body doesn't know the difference between real or fake laughter. Therefore, even by practising fake laughter, you can receive the same great physical and psychological benefits as when laughing for real.

One way you can start practising fake laughter is by rhythmically reciting and repeating the following laughter-phrase: "ho, ho, ha ha ha!" whilst clapping in steady time. Using musical notation, this method looks like this:

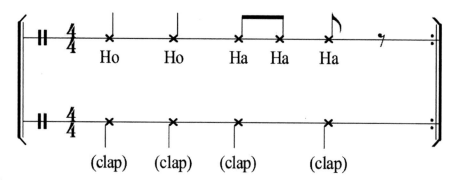

You can of course come up with your own variations to get you started.

If you are in the company of others who are also willing to try this technique, firstly check that you are in a location where it might be appropriate to launch into fits of Laughing Yoga! Then stand facing each other in a circle, and make sure you all have good eye contact with each other. Begin by using the "ho, ho, ha ha ha!" starter given above.

When practising, your fake or forced laughter quickly becomes real, and especially so when making eye contact with others in a group situation. By yourself it can be more of a challenge, but it is possible!

By practising Laughing Yoga, you are reinforcing positive thought processes, relieving psychological stress, and improving your overall level of physical condition. The benefits of Laughing Yoga can be highly conducive to optimising your level of performance arousal, thereby giving you easier and more enjoyable access to The Zone.

19. Learn to Laugh at Yourself

Some of us have the tendency to beat ourselves up psychologically because we don't perform exactly as we would like to either in the practise room or in the performance arena. Remember however, that as a performer you are striving to achieve a goal which is unachievable in many fields of performance – perfection! If your performance doesn't go exactly as you expect, or even if it is a complete 'crash and burn', beating yourself up about it is not going to change the situation!

It happens to everyone sooner or later

The reality is that we all fail to some extent at some time in our lives. Even the greatest performers in the world will undoubtedly have a nightmare story or two – whether they are willing to share these stories or not. It is therefore reasonable to assume that at some time in your life you might not perform exactly 100% as you had planned. That is called life! And without life, you're dead – so get over it!!

By learning to genuinely laugh at yourself when things don't go your way is a great tool for silencing that spoiled brat inside of all of us – the ego. Now I'm not saying that you should go out there into the performance arena with the express intention of failing, just so that you can laugh at yourself! But if things don't go completely your way, being able to sit back and find something funny in the situation can be a great help.

Getting back on the horse

In extreme cases, it may seem like your situation is completely ludicrous, and that if you didn't laugh, you'd probably cry. Both laughing and crying are a very similar form of emotional release – laughing is just a lot more fun!

And you can laugh at yourself whenever you like! You need to be aware that learning to laugh at yourself is a great way of getting back on the horse, instead of slapping yourself in the face with a wet fish because you fell off!

Medical benefits

In addition, the medical benefits of laughter have been well documented by several studies in recent years, and include an activation of the immune system, a decrease in stress hormones, a relaxing effect on muscles, a perceived reduction of pain, regulation of blood pressure, and a cleansing of the respiratory system. Laughing even offers a form of mild cardiac exercise. Side-effect free and available to all free of charge, laughter really can be 'the best medicine'. Given its therapeutic effects, being able to laugh at yourself, practising Laughing Yoga as explained in the previous chapter, and simply laughing in general, can be enjoyable techniques to use in your journey to The Zone.

85

20. Living in The Now

All too often, many of us are excessively concerned with what will happen in the future, and how things were in the past, that we forget to live here and now. Planning for the future and enjoying previous successes are both important. However living in the future or in the past can cause some serious problems, especially when this time thinking about the future is actually time worrying about the future, and the time thinking of the past is actually time regurgitating and reliving old negative memories.

The past

When living in the past, the mentality is often, "Back then it was easier", or "Back then there were more opportunities", or "So and so said this to me and it made me feel bad", or "I should've done that", or "I regret doing that", or "If I had only done this one thing, my life would be better now" – the examples are endless.

The significance of the past

The past does have a certain amount of significance in our lives, but there is absolutely nothing you or anyone else can do to change the past. Nothing. Accepting the fact that you do not live in the past, rather, you live here and in this very moment, is a mind set which can, if fully comprehended, be an extremely liberating state.

Some might argue that the events in your past make up who you are. This is not entirely true. It is how you dealt with the events in your past that makes up who you are. We have all had both good and bad experiences in the past. However it is our perception of these events – how we cherished, acknowledged and savoured the good, and how we dealt with, learned from, understood, and moved on from the bad – that make the difference.

"The past does not equal the future"

The motivational psychologist Tony Robbins states that "the past does not equal the future." Is he right? Decide for yourself. Have you ever heard of a rags-to-riches story? About someone who had no job, no money, maybe even no place to live, but succeeded in life anyway? This person took specific actions, became successful, broke the negative cycle of the past, created a better present for themselves, and opened up a more promising future.

Some contemporary performers proving that the past doesn't equal the future include Haile Gebrselassie (middle and long distance runner, and breaker of 26 world records), Madonna (international pop artist), Gordon Ramsay (master chef and television personality), Sidney Poitier (actor), Erik von Markovik aka. 'Mystery' (master pickup artist), and Tony Robbins (life coach and motivational speaker).

Motivation from a difficult past

In fact, many of the greatest performers came from a background of poverty or some other form of hardship. Many of them were dissatisfied with their current situation, and used this as intense motivation to make a change and become the best in their field. Some found the personal motivation because they simply refused to continue in their current life situation. Others wanted to ensure that their children would never have to suffer the same hardships that they themselves experienced whilst growing up. The more pessimistic person might say, "But yeah, that was them, it was just luck, they were in the right place at the right time, they got a lucky break, it doesn't happen like that for everyone – especially not me!" And of course that pessimistic person is completely correct!

But wait, does this sound like a contradiction? The past doesn't equal the future AND the past does equal the future? No. The past only equals the future when you decide, consciously or subconsciously, that that's the way it is and will always be. Contrarily, the past does not equal the future if you decide, consciously or subconsciously, that this is the case.

The past in perspective

The point here is that your life in the past has a certain amount of importance – but not nearly as much importance as your life here and now. Most of us place a certain importance on looking back occasionally at our successes and achievements to remind ourselves that we are successful people. There is nothing wrong with this at all. However it could be argued that it is equally as important for us to occasionally look back at the less productive or happy times, and ask ourselves the following questions: What did I learn from that experience? How has that experience helped me in my life?

We have all had failures and successes, bad and good experiences, problems and solutions, and hurt and joy in our past for one simple reason: To teach us something. Learn from your past, and you win!

The future

How will things be in your life tomorrow? Next week? Next month? Next year? In 2 years? In 5 years? In 10 years? In 20 years? Some might think they know what will happen in the near future – maybe the coming weeks or months. Some people may even think they know how their lives will be in several years time.

However the fact of the matter is that no one knows exactly how things will be in the future – not a single person. We can take educated guesses, or have a plan or intent, but there are absolutely no guarantees. This doesn't mean that we shouldn't make plans, or shouldn't have intent. Neither does it mean that we should be worried about the uncertainty of our possible futures. It simply means that when we make plans, we need to be flexible enough to accept that they might not always turn out as we hoped, and that is completely okay.

The worrier

There are basically two ways of thinking about known future challenges or trying events, and neither should be dwelled upon to any extent. The first way is simply worry, or anxiety.

When given a performance task on a specific date, the worrier will concentrate on how difficult the task is and the problems associated with it. The worrier feels a sense of overwhelm, preventing any action from taking place. With the deadline getting ever closer, the cycle of worry intensifies and may even turn to panic. This panic, in many worriers, spurs an onslaught of last-minute action, leaving the worrier exhausted and of course under-prepared physically and mentally for the task at hand. This most often results in a level of performance far below the worrier's true potential.

The doer

The doer on the other hand may initially sense the same basic feeling surrounding the impending performance. However the doer uses this energy in a different way. Instead of being self-destructive, the doer sets wheels in motion instantaneously by concentrating on solutions and taking action which will, all other things being equal, result in a higher level of performance that is better reflective of their true potential as a performer.

Here and now

Life, and therefore performing, takes place neither in the past nor the future – it takes place here, and now. In the past, your life, and your performances took place in the now of the past. In the future, your life and your performances will take place in the now of the future. But for this very moment, your life is happening right now. And that is why *the now*, is the best, and only place in the world.

The best and only place in the world – the now

Your life is taking place in one place and one place only – and that place is called *the now*. By completely enjoying, savouring and immersing yourself in the experience of what is happening right now, it is by logic impossible to be affected by the events of the past or the uncertainties of the future. When you are 100% focussed, 100% caught-up in the moment, you are living and being here in *the now*. And by doing this, you are simultaneously letting go of the past and ignoring the future.

In the moment

Children at play are a perfect example of living in the here and now. They can become completely caught up in the game, where neither the past nor the future is given any thought energy whatsoever. Predatory animals stalking their prey are another great example. They are completely caught up in the moment, neither conscious of the past nor the uncertainty of the future – their minds arguably incapable of harbouring thoughts of "what if" and "remember way back when."

Focussing on the now

The power of accepting that you do not know what will happen in the future, and completely and utterly letting go of control by accepting this state of not knowing, helps to concentrate your focus on *the now*. It is *the now* that is taking place and of relevance. How you performed 5 years ago, 1 year ago, 1 month ago, yesterday, or even 1 minute ago does not necessarily need to have any bearing on how you perform *right now* unless you decide consciously or subconsciously that it does.

Performing, and the now

Contemplating the outcome of your performance, or thinking that you have knowledge about how the outcome of your performance will affect you, is not conducive to a successful performance. In fact, this is the primary cause for the negative manifestation of performance arousal, or performance anxiety. When concentrating on the outcome of a performance, your ego takes over, giving the negatively charged "What if" statements a greater chance of resounding in your consciousness.

Imagine that you could live only in *the now* when on the performing stage. If you could achieve this state, it would be impossible not to achieve an optimum level of performance. In other words, if you can only live in this very moment by practising living in the here and now, you can instantly achieve optimal performance arousal and reach The Zone in any performing situation. That is the power of living here and now.

Practising the Alexander Technique, mentioned in Chapter 40, is one way of living in *the now* in daily life and performing situations alike. Studying the teachings of Eckhart Tolle (see Bibliography and Suggested Further Reading) will also give you a deeper insight on *the now* and how to achieve this state.

Once you have a sense of *the now*, simply writing the words *"the now"* on a Cue Card may be all that is required to help you trigger this state of being purely in The Zone.

21. My Time, and Intelligent Time Management

How much time do you spend in the average day completely by yourself? Time when you are undisturbed, without ringing telephones or text messages, time without emails to read and reply to, time without other people or electronic devices requiring your attention? How much quality time do you have each day for the most important person in your world? Who is the most important person in your world by the way? The answer is you! Because without you, your world wouldn't exist!

My Time

Setting aside a certain period of the day for My Time can be a liberating and rejuvenating experience for anyone, especially performers living in high-stress, fast-paced environments. For some, the most suitable period of the day for My Time is just before bed, for others it is first thing in the morning, or perhaps during a suitable break in the middle of the day. All of us, regardless of our performance sphere, can benefit from at least a short period of My Time for inner reflection, peace, and calm, every single day.

When taking your well deserved My Time, you may opt to walk outside in a natural environment, such as on a beach or in a forest. Alternatively you may simply choose to sit or lay down on a comfortable sofa. Make sure you turn off all electronic devices, including mobile phones, computers, the television, and so on.

My Time with questions

During your My Time, you may also like to ponder over some empowering questions, such as:

• What am I most thankful/grateful for in my life right now?
• What is it that is truly important in my life?
• How far have I progressed in the past year/years?
• What achievements/successes have I had?
• How have I grown, and what have I learned over the past months/year/years?

The added bonus of asking positively charged questions such as those above, should you decide to do adopt this strategy, is that you allow yourself the chance to come up with positive answers.

My Time without questions

Alternatively, when practising and enjoying your period of My Time, you may simply like to relax, clear your mind, and think of nothing – letting your thoughts wander freely, letting them come and go.

How much time

The amount of My Time you require may vary from only a few minutes per day, up to as much as an hour, or even more. If you find yourself without a single minute to yourself, a constant slave to the demands of electronic devices or other people, then you must create a sacred period of My Time at some point in your day. But how is this done, especially given our hectic modern schedules? Cue Intelligent Time Management.

Intelligent Time Management

By far the best way to 'create' time is to control it. You have, whether you realise it or not, an amazing capacity to control a large amount of your own time. Some philosophers may even say that you have complete control over your time, 24 hours per day, 7 days per week, regardless of your personal circumstances. Others will argue that time simply does not exist. Philosophical discussions aside for a moment, let's discuss a simple way where you can effectively 'create' more time in your daily life.

Timetabling

Firstly, if you don't already have a detailed schedule or timetable for the week, make one! A timetable can be a very simple document, with days of the week listed at the top, and hours of the day listed in a column on the left. Fill in your fixed compulsory engagements, (including sleep and meal breaks!) in the spaces in the timetable. This can give you a clear and instantaneous overview of how you utilise the hours in your day.

You may feel inner resistance to creating a timetable for yourself, as it may seem over simplistic or perhaps even childish. You may even try to convince yourself that you don't have time for this! However the more resistance you feel towards making and following a timetable, the stronger the likelihood may be that you do in fact require it. Try it for a month, and judge for yourself how much time you are able to utilise more efficiently. A sample timetable is given on the next page.

A sample timetable

Sample	Monday	Tuesday	Wednesday	Thursday	Friday	Saturday	Sunday
07.00	My Time + Free Writing	My Time + Free Writing	My Time + Free Writing	My Time + Free Writing	My Time + Free Writing	Sleep	Sleep
08.00	Morning prep.	Morning prep.	Morning prep.	Morning prep.	Morning prep.	Sleep	Sleep
09.00	Travel			Travel		Sleep	Sleep
10.00	Drama school	Travel		Drama school		Sleep	Morning prep.
11.00	Drama school	Drama school		Drama school	Travel	My Time + Free Writing	Travel
12.00	Lunch	Lunch	Lunch	Lunch		Morning prep.	Work
13.00	Drama school	Drama school	Travel	Drama school	Lunch		Work
14.00		Drama school	Drama school	Drama school	Drama school	Lunch	Lunch
15.00	Drama school	Drama school	Drama school		Travel	Travel	Work
16.00				Drama school		Work	Work
17.00	Dinner	Dinner	Drama school	Drama school		Work	Work
18.00	Drama school	Drama school	Travel	Travel	Travel		
19.00	Drama school	Drama school	Dinner	Dinner			Travel
20.00	Travel	Travel			Travel	Travel	Dinner
21.00					Night out	Dinner	My Time
22.00					Night out		Sleep
23.00	Sleep	Sleep	Sleep	Sleep	Night out till late	Sleep	Sleep

Using this example, you can quickly see that even this busy drama student has several free hours during the course of a week. By isolating their free time, they are then able to schedule periods during the week when other techniques given in this book could be practised.

The Grand Master Time Thief

By creating your own timetable, you too may find that you have many more free hours in a week than you originally thought. But where has all of this time 'gone' previously? Non-compulsory engagements such as T.V. watching, video game playing, or possibly even recovering from hangovers could provide some answers. When it comes to non-compulsory engagements, try to ask yourself the following: "What results am I achieving by doing this?"

The television for example, one of the most revolutionary but unfortunately over-used and taken for granted inventions of the 20ᵗʰ century, is a vice many people employ which could easily be given the esteemed title Grand Master Time Thief.

If you find yourself with little or no time in your week for My Time, but yet have several non-compulsory engagements including serving the Grand Master Time Thief for several hours each week, it may be time for some priority changes! Start by throwing the T.V. out of the window! Or, less dramatically, lock it up in the attic for a while, and enjoy the extra time and freedom you have now created for yourself!

This way, instead of filling the 'computer' between your ears with unnecessary data by watching hours of 'reality' shows and the like (the word 'reality' being used rather lightly here), you could try the ultimately more rewarding, liberating, and refreshing art of releasing your own on thoughts on paper by employing the technique of Free Writing, as explained earlier in Chapter 13.

21

21. Exercise: Intelligent Time Management

Create and follow a timetable, incorporating a period of My Time every day. In this way, you can make the best use of the one commodity that we all have in common – time.

Your timetable

	Monday	Tuesday	Wednesday	Thursday	Friday	Saturday	Sunday
07.00							
08.00							
09.00							
10.00							
11.00							
12.00							
13.00							
14.00							
15.00							
16.00							
17.00							
18.00							
19.00							
20.00							
21.00							
22.00							
23.00							

22. Posture, Body Language, and Movement

Your posture, how you move your body, and the subconscious signals telegraphed to others via your body language, are inextricably linked to your emotional state, your perception of any given situation, your own sense of self worth, and the worth that you perceive in those around you. You can tell if a person is insecure or unsure of themselves simply by how they sit, stand, move their body, and use their face. Likewise you know if a person is confident simply by how they stand, gesture, and move across a room.

95

A comfortable and secure person, completely at ease with himself or herself and confident with their own abilities, inadvertently sends powerful non-verbal signals to those around them. This can be observed at any public gathering. Simply compare a 'wall flower' to the 'life of the party' and you will see the powerful effects of posture, body language, and movement.

The mind/body connection

Your emotional state and your body language are complimentary. That is, your state of mind affects your posture and body movement, just as posture and body movement affects your state of mind. Therefore, understanding and exerting conscious control over your posture and body movement can affect your mental state, which in turn has a direct impact on the level of performance arousal you experience.

A negative cycle

If you move your body in short, quick, erratic, stiff, and more or less uncontrolled motions, you are most likely experiencing anxiety – the negative manifestation of performance arousal – or are well on your way to being there. In this situation, you not only make yourself feel ill at ease, but you also communicate this distress to others, who will more than likely communicate to you (perhaps on a less subtle level) that they would rather not find themselves in your immediate vicinity. Receiving this negative communication from others can then reinforce negative performance arousal, creating a powerful cycle of distress and anxiety.

Breaking the cycle

Some performers are constantly caught up in this cycle, which can become an inherent part of who they are and how they act in everyday situations, affecting not only how they perform, but their social interactions as well. If this sounds a little too familiar, you must take steps to break this cycle! By consciously changing the way in which you move your body, you can exert an influence over your psychological state, which can thereby be perceived by others as being attractive, rather than repulsive. This reaction from others again can lead to a greater sense of confidence, positive reinforcement, and can thereby strengthen the cycle of positive posture, body language and movement.

Different types of movement

Posture and body movement is fundamental in all of the Eastern martial arts and this is no different in global performance arenas. By simply moving your body in a deliberate, relaxed, flowing, and gentle way, such as in Qi Gong or Tai Chi, you can induce a state of physical and mental calm, control, and at the same time alertness, and can achieve a performance arousal level of 0 or +1 on the performance arousal scale. Slow body movement can be a perfect antidote for performers who often find themselves 'over-hyped', at the positive side of the performance arousal scale, or panicky and anxious, at the negative end of the performance arousal scale.

By executing relaxed yet strong, controlled, deliberate, movements, your body and mind can be activated and optimised for a moderate level of positive performance arousal, perhaps +2 or +3.

And of course by activating your body in large, extravagant, confident, swift, and powerful movements with an unmistakeable sense of purpose, such as professional wrestlers prior to and during matches, you can activate a +4 or even +5 performance arousal level.

For certain performing situations, the use of a Cue Card can give a quick and potent reminder for you of posture, body language, and movement.

22. Exercise: Watch and learn

When you are next in a social situation, observe the posture, body language and body movement of those around you. Can you differentiate between those people who are most comfortable, confident, and fully at ease with themselves and the situation, and those people who are least comfortable, confident, and unsure of themselves, purely by reading their body language?

Note the body language of the less comfortable, less confident people. Can you identify something that they are doing with their bodies, expressions, or gestures that you could avoid doing prior to, or during a performance situation?

97

_____

_____

_____

_____

_____

_____

_____

Now look at the body language of the more comfortable, more confident people. Can you identify something that they are doing with their bodies, expressions, or gestures that you could possibly adopt prior to, or during a performance situation?

`22`

_____

_____

_____

_____

_____

_____

Try adopting one or more of these comfortable, confident body motions or postures in your next practise session or performance, if appropriate. How does your practise or performance improve when taking on this posture or carrying out this motion?

_____

_____

_____

_____

_____

_____

This exercise, related to role modelling in Chapter 27, can have a profound effect on the level of performance arousal you experience. Improving your body language, posture and the quality of your physical movement can help you to optimise your level of performance arousal, getting you closer to performing in The Zone.

23. Practise!

It is unlikely that simply reading about and understanding these techniques and exercises will help you to any great extent in your journey to The Zone. The techniques and exercises in this book must be **practised** in order for you to gain the maximum benefits!

Practise makes perfect?

Most of us are familiar with the phrase, "Practise makes perfect." However this adage can at times be a little misleading. Perhaps the phrase should be extended to, "Practise leads to improvement in the action that you are carrying out, whether that action is correct or not." Not quite as catchy, but perhaps a little more correct!

Correct practise

If you complete an action enough times, the chances are that you will become better at carrying out that action. If the action is helpful, positive, 'correct', and conducive to your improvement as a performer, then the first phrase, "Practise makes perfect", is more or less true.

Incorrect practise

But what happens if the action that you are practising is 'incorrect', and actually has a negative effect on yourself or your ability to perform? The same rules apply of course. That is, you will more than likely become more astute at carrying out this incorrect action. In other words, by practising incorrectly, you will unfortunately get better at doing things incorrectly.

A new practise phrase

This phrase taught to me by my mentor, John Lauderdale, explains the psychology of the effects of practise in a more neutral, eloquent and accurate manner: "Whatever you do the most of, that's what you'll be best at." As with practising an instrument, learning your lines, training your body, or learning your steps, tools and techniques such as the ones presented here in Part Two: The Techniques, should be practised regularly, diligently, and the exercises carried out as prescribed – to the best of your ability.

Momentum

An ancient Chinese proverb, accredited to Lao Tzu states, "A journey of a thousand miles begins with a single step." Therefore, in order to build the best possible momentum in your journey to The Zone, you must take at least **one small positive action every day!** Consistency here is the key.

The day you made the decision to purchase this book can be considered a positive action. The days spent reading and understanding this book can be considered further small steps in the right direction. Time spent practising the techniques in this part of *Performing in The Zone* are of course vital positive actions. And finally, taking rest when earned, and breaks when needed, is also a valuable part of the process of building momentum.

By experimenting with the individual techniques given in this book and applying them regularly, you can gain momentum in your journey to The Zone. Once you've had some practise with the individual techniques in this part of *Performing in The Zone*, perhaps the most efficient and surest way to gain further momentum is to begin (and complete!) The 12 Week Performance Success Programme, explained in Part Three: The Programme.

24. Practising Performing – 5 Steps to Mastery

We practise our instruments, the steps, our lines, our expressions or body language. We learn the exercises, the rules, and the strategies of the game. We go through the motions in our practise room, at home, in the car, at the rehearsal hall or training grounds. As long as we practise correctly, we improve in our chosen field of performance.

Crash and burn

But how often do we actually get the chance to practise the performance itself? Some performers beat themselves up mentally because despite extensive rehearsals, practise sessions or training, their performance arousal level resulted in a massive "crash and burn." But wait a second. If this same performer hasn't actually practised performing don't you think he or she is being a little unfair on himself or herself? Have you ever found yourself in this situation maybe? Performing without practising the art of performing is like walking with your eyes closed. It might be okay for a short while but sooner or later you're probably going to hit something and it could very well be painful! Therefore, practising performing (just as important as walking with your eyes open) is a must for any serious performer to avoid "crash and burn" and to get used to performing in The Zone.

A better alternative

With the specialised technique of Practising Performing – 5 Steps to Mastery, you start off by practising how to perform in positive, low pressure situations, with nothing to lose. You build up gently, by getting used to situations with gradually increasing amounts of pressure, and becoming accustomed to giving real performances with an ideal level of performance arousal. You may choose to practise this particular technique as a part of The 12 Week Performance Success Programme, explained in Part Three of *Performing in The Zone*, or choose to adopt Practising Performing – 5 Steps to Mastery, as a separate exercise.

Here's how it works

The technique of Practising Performing – 5 Steps to Mastery, should be carried out over a 5 week period, with each step lasting for a full week. At the end of the 5th week you conclude Practising Performing – 5 Steps to Mastery by giving a real performance. You may choose to start with this technique exactly 5 weeks before a scheduled public performance, or, organise a private performance. Your performance at the end of the 5 week period can be as elaborate as an international competition or as humble as a simple, short demonstration for close friends, family, or colleagues.

Before you start this technique, it is best to be more or less on top of your performance programme. That is to say that you should already be reasonably familiar with your lines, repertoire, steps, or performance event before you start. Go through the following 5 steps, and chart your progress using the performance journal template provided at Appendix 2, your own hard-backed book with blank pages or journal, or word-processing program on a computer.

Step 1:   Practise Performing in Your Mind

With this first gentle step, you will begin to practise performing in your mind only. That is, you will go through a purely imagined rehearsal of your performance, or even just one part of it, using your mind's eye only.

To begin, stand or sit in your practise environment, with your instrument, props, notes or equipment if applicable. Take the time you require to get comfortable. When you are ready, close your eyes.

Imagine that you are carrying out your performance, or part of it, exactly as you want it to sound/look in as much detail as possible. It is important that you imagine your performance in real time – that is, in the actual time it takes to go through your performance. Start at the beginning of your piece/scene/event/speech. Perform in your mind exactly as you would like to perform in a performance environment. Do this without playing a note, uttering a word, taking a step, or making any physical gestures. Imagine you are there, in the performance arena, doing a great job, and enjoying the moment.
Enjoy the freedom that an effortless, ideal performance in your mind gives you. Keep imagining your performance exactly as you want it to be, until it is over.

Carry out this exercise at least once, but preferably twice or even three times per day if time allows. Practising performing in your mind can be done in addition to your regular practise for a full week. For many performers, continuing this step for the entire lead up to a performance can be extremely beneficial.

If your sphere of performance is physically very demanding, practising performing in your mind can have the added bonus of doubling your productivity, whilst halving your physical effort. When interspersing this technique with actual practise, the results can be extremely powerful.

Remember to practise this step **every day** if possible, in the most vivid detail you can imagine, and in real time.

Record your results and observations in your performance journal.

Step 2: Practise Performing by Yourself

In Step 2 you will need to set up your practise or rehearsal space so that it resembles a performance space as much as possible. For example, shift some chairs and tables near a wall to emulate where a possible jury or audience might sit, if appropriate for your performing situation. Also, by adjusting lighting if possible, you can provide an added touch of realism.

When the room or performance space is ready, turn off your mobile phone! And make sure you won't be disturbed by anyone else for the time it will take you to go through your performance programme.

103

Now, leave the room or performance space.

Wait outside for 1 – 5 minutes.

This is a perfect time to experiment with Pre-Performance Rituals, Mantras, or other techniques in this book to get your performance arousal level to where it needs to be. This is also an ideal time to practise using Cue Cards.

When you are ready, re-enter the performance space as if it was your performance day.

Take the time you need in the room or performance space before you start (if appropriate) to enable you to deliver your best possible performance.

Begin your performance and run it through from beginning to end without stopping! If something doesn't go quite right do not go back and fix it. This is a performance! If you do stop, you are defeating the purpose of the exercise. Just keep going no matter what happens! Remember where on the performance arousal scale you want to be.

When you have finished, leave the room or performance space again. Yes, leave!

Now your performance is complete.

24

Complete Step 2 **once per day** if possible for a full week. If your performance programme is physically demanding, do Step 2 anyway! However, depending on how physically demanding your performance programme is, you may choose to omit different sections each time you practise this step. Another strategy with physically demanding performances is to alternate between Step 1 and Step 2 on different days, taking complete days off if required.

The idea here is to build up gently. Take special care that the more strenuous your performance programme, the longer and more crucial your rest periods become. Do not over do it! Remember to keep a record of this week in your performance journal.

Step 3:   Practise Performing to a Recording Device

Set up a portable video camera in your practise space. Alternatively, you can use an audio recording device such as a mini-disc player, if appropriate. Prepare the performance space as you did in Step 2. If you are indoors, you may like to try with different furniture placements, or perhaps you could try standing/sitting in a different part of the room, facing another direction, or even using a different performance space altogether if available. Variation can be helpful here. When the performance space is ready, press the record button, and leave the room.

Go through the same process as in Step 2. Make sure you run your performance from beginning to end as if it was the day of your event – that is, without stopping. When you are finished, leave the performance arena. Re-enter, and then turn off your recorder.

Should you watch/listen to your recording?

If by viewing/hearing your recording you will be able to enjoy and savour the good parts of your performance, and constructively assess and learn from the aspects that require more attention, then yes! However if you don't feel totally comfortable reviewing your performance, try waiting a few days before deciding to watch/listen to your recording. There are no hard and fast rules here. Remember that you can always delete your recordings whenever you choose. And who knows? Maybe practising performing to a recording device will provide some great material for your next promotional video or audition tape!

Again, repeat this step **every day** for a week, taking rests when required.

Keep your performance journal up to date.

Step 4: Practise Performing to Close Friends or Colleagues

After a week of Step 1 – Practise Performing in Your Mind, a week of Step 2 – Practise Performing by Yourself, and a week of Step 3 – Practise Performing to a Recording Device, performing should start to feel more familiar and comfortable. Do make sure that your experiences during this entire process are as constructive as possible, and do take days off to rest if you feel it is necessary!

Review where you were 3 weeks ago and compare that to now by asking yourself the **105** following questions:

How much have I achieved over the past 3 weeks?
What have I learned over the past 3 weeks?
Which areas of my performance am I most happy with?
Which areas need more work?
Which Mantra or other Pre-Performance Rituals work best for me?

This week, to practise Step 4, you will need to gather together a small group of friends or colleagues to hear/see you perform. As an alternative, performing to a group of pre-school children, students, or even adults that have no relation to your performance sphere can offer a realistic yet constructive practise environment for you.

Ask your chosen audience to assemble at your performance location at a specific time. Set up the performance space accordingly before they arrive. When the performance time comes, wait outside the room until you are ready to enter, as you have done in previous steps. Go through any Mantra or Pre-Performance Rituals you may have. When ready, enter the room, introduce your performance if appropriate, and begin.

Enjoy the contact you now have with your real-life audience. Carry out your performance from beginning to end, and again leave the performance space when you are finished. The performance is now complete. Re-enter the room and enjoy the company!

You may choose to ask your audience for constructive comments, or simply request that they refrain from giving opinions. Again, there are no fixed rules here. In practising performing to close friends or colleagues, it can also be useful to use a recorder as in Step 3.

You may choose to utilise Step 4 perhaps once, twice or even several times throughout the course of this week. Remember, in the case of more demanding performances you do not have to perform your entire programme. Simply perform as little or as much as you wish.

You may choose to mention that you are giving an abridged version of your performance in your welcome speech to your audience, if appropriate.

Chart your progress in your performance journal!

Worst Case Scenario – No Holds Barred!

As a variation on Step 4: Practise Performing to Close Friends or Colleagues, you may ask your audience to employ the Worst Case Scenario – No Holds Barred! technique of performer distraction.

When using this technique, encourage your audience to distract you during your performance. Ask them to be creative!

One suggestion for using this technique is to experiment with it three times during the course of a week. On your first performance to your real life audience, you may ask them to be mildly distracting. Perhaps coughing at inappropriate moments, and even ringing mobile phones during your performance will do. On a second performance, you may encourage your audience to engage in loud conversation, as well as asking them to enter and leave the room during your performance. For the grand finale third performance, tell your audience that they can do whatever they like (as long as they don't make physical contact with you) to try to distract you.

The idea here is that you gradually become accustomed to external distractions, which end up being perceived as completely ridiculous. Maintaining your focus in such a ludicrous performance environment will almost certainly help you to keep focussed, should there be less dramatic external interference during your actual performance in Step 5: Practising Performing.

Step 5:   Practising Performing

You've now completed four full weeks of practising performing. You know which aspects of your performing that you're most happy with, and you know which aspects need some extra work.

In this final step, you have the real performance as a goal at the end of this week. In the days leading up to this performance, you may choose to decide on one specific Mantra or Pre-Performance Ritual to focus on. You can also use these final days for any last minute polishing of a performance programme, for some light training to keep yourself in shape without making you physically tired, or to simply rest, if appropriate.

As a performer, we strive for perfection – an elusive goal. In some fields of performance you can even argue that perfection by definition is impossible to achieve. However excellence and improvement are very real goals. By being true to this technique, Practising Performing – 5 Steps to Mastery, you may be one, if not several steps closer to excellence, an optimal level of performance arousal, and closer to The Zone. You could even be there already.

By the time your real performance day comes, you know the routine. You've done it all before – many times. Using Practising Performing – 5 Steps to Mastery, you have gradually built yourself up one step at a time.

As with any aspect of being a performer, every practise session you undertake is a learning opportunity. The same goes for performing. As the famous musical theatre song states, "The sun will come out tomorrow." There will always be future performances. Why not use this current performance as just another training session for your next performance? What can you learn from it?

If you complete this exercise, Practising Performing – 5 Steps to Mastery, and learn or discover only one thing about yourself, improve only one aspect of your performance, or make even a slight improvement in the appropriateness of your performance arousal level, you have gone in the right direction towards optimal performance – you are on the right path to performing in The Zone. Keep going!

Review the 5 steps of this Practising Performing for your next major performance. How can you improve this process? How can your performance practising be even more rewarding?

And finally, remember this: moving gradually forward is so much better than going full-speed in reverse! Be patient and enjoy the process – you can make it happen!

25. Pre-Performance Rituals and Mantras

Pre-Performance Rituals are designed to trigger the exact performance arousal level you require for any given performance situation, putting you immediately in The Zone. Although often a technique commonly associated with athletes, Pre-Performance Rituals can be highly useful for all performers.

One example - the haka

One of the most powerful and effective examples of Pre-Performance Rituals is carried out by the All Blacks – the New Zealand national rugby team. Rugby is an intensely physical team sport, requiring strength and stamina, a high level of skill, speed, tactics, and fearlessness. On the performance arousal scale it often rates around +4 and +5.

The traditional Maori war dance called the *haka* is performed by the All Blacks in front of the opposing team as a Pre-Performance Ritual prior to every game. The haka can not only induce fear in the opposition, but is also a tool which invokes an immediate +4 or +5 response in the players performing it. This traditional Maori war dance is perhaps one of the 'secrets' of the All Blacks' unprecedented international success in the rugby world.

A Sample Mantra: C3

Although "doing the haka" to gain a +5 level of performance arousal prior to a performance is perhaps inappropriate for many performers, there are other equally effective Pre-Performance Rituals available which can just as effectively bring about lower activation levels of the positive manifestation of performance arousal. One that I have personally used to great effect is a Mantra that I call C3.

Prior to important performances in recent years I've written the figure C3 in small print on the upper-side of my right hand, at the base of my thumb and forefinger. (This area of the hand is positioned almost directly in front of the face when playing the trumpet.) As an alternative to writing on your hand, you may choose to use a Cue Card, as mentioned earlier in this chapter.

Calm, confident, controlled

C3 for me stands for calm, confident, and controlled. Using this technique I think of the word "calm" and the feeling associated with the word "calm" as I take a gentle breath in and out. I repeat the process for "confident", and again for "controlled". This Mantra is something I use to quickly bring my naturally high performance arousal level down to a +1. For situations that require +2, you might like to use D3 – drive, determination, destiny. A +3 situation might be F3 – funky, fun, free. Abbreviations such as these can be invaluable reminders for you prior to, or even during performances.

Chapter 25

25a. Exercise: Create your own Mantra

Create a Mantra for your own performance purposes.

An Example:

My Mantra: C3
This means: "calm, confident, controlled"
                Breathe in and out for each word, focussing on the meaning of the word

Your Mantra: _____

This means: _____

_____

_____

Other Pre-Performance Rituals

As a performer, you may like to invent a certain phrase to recite, or come up with a special physical movement that you can carry out before entering the performance space to help you get into an ideal state of mind for your performance. Your Pre-Performance Ritual can be subtle such as C3, extreme such as the *haka*, or something in between, such as simply 'putting on your game face'.

As an alternative, you may like to experiment with different scents, or wearing certain colours to help get you into The Zone. You could even put on your lucky underwear the morning of a performance! The rule here is, if it works for you, do it!

25b. Exercise: Create some Pre-Performance Rituals

Come up with three Pre-Performance Rituals that you can experiment with to help bring you into an ideal state of mind for your performing situations. e.g. Wear special piece of clothing

1.   _____

_____

2.   _____

_____

3.   _____

_____

26. Qi Gong – A Soft Style Martial Art

Some of us tend to naturally experience high levels of performance arousal in performing situations and may have difficulty becoming relaxed, calm, and grounded in situations requiring composure, poise, and control. The following exercise is excellent for obtaining a sense of stillness, calm, or a feeling of being centred as some like to describe it. It is a basic Qi Gong exercise, executable by all and ideal for calming the mind and body, helping obtain low levels of positive performance arousal, ideal for performers requiring fine control of motor skills.

Disclaimer: The information given below is in no way intended to replace specialist medical advice provided by a health professional. Should you suspect that you have a health problem you should visit a health professional immediately.

Basic Horse-stance Standing Meditation

There are several variations on the horse-stance, all used for different purposes. For the purpose of basic standing meditation as a means of controlling performance arousal, the stance below is recommended.

1. Preferably barefoot, stand with both of your feet flat on the floor, shoulder width apart. Men should stand with feet parallel. Women may also stand with feet parallel, or alternatively, pointed outwards at an angle of approximately 30 – 45 degrees. Feel where your feet make contact with the floor. Lightly grip the floor with your toes. Feel the stability and balance near the arch of your foot.

2. Bend your knees very slightly so that they are directly over your toes. Your heels, hips, and shoulders should be in a straight vertical line. Let your arms hang loosely by your sides. Keep your hands relaxed and soft.

3. Imagine there is a string at the crown of your head gently pulling your head upward. Tuck in your chin very slightly. At the same time, tuck your pelvis under and forward, minimising the curvature in your lower spine. Relax.

4. Turn the palms of your hands out to face the front. Let your fingers keep their relaxed, natural position. Half-close your eyes. Gently press your tongue to the hard palate behind your teeth. Keep your tongue here whilst breathing gently through the nose for the duration of the exercise.

5.   The area approximately 2-3 cm below the navel is often referred to as the *dan tien* (lower elixir field) or *qi hai* (sea of energy). With every breath in, imagine energy flowing from this point through your body to the base of your spine, and then up your spine to the crown of your head. With each breath out, imagine the energy flowing back down the front of your body to your *dan tien*, completing the loop. Breathe slowly and smoothly through your nose, both on the in and out breath.

6.   After a minute or so, take a half step to the side with your left leg. Turn your palms so that they are facing each other, and slowly raise your arms so that they are approximately parallel to the ground, directly in front of you, and shoulder width apart. Make sure the centres of your palms, the *lao gung* points, are facing. Curve your fingers inwards slightly, keeping them naturally lightly spread. Relax.

7. With every breath in, gently pull your arms apart slightly, keeping your palms directly facing one another. On every breath out, bring your arms back to shoulder width. Imagine you are stretching and contracting a rubber band between your palms. Feel the energy between your hands.

8. Focus. Concentrate on feeling the energy flowing from your *dan tien*, up your spine to the crown of your head, and down the front of your body back to the *dan tien*. Feel the energy flowing between the *lao gung* points of your palms. Breathe in through the nose. Breathe out through the nose.

9. Continue step 7 and 8 for approximately 3 – 5 minutes.

10. When you are ready to continue, raise your arms slowly to a vertical position above your head, hands still shoulder width apart, palms still facing. Now spread your arms out wide so that they are almost parallel with the floor. Your palms should now be facing upwards. Tilt your head slightly back.

11. Bring your arms parallel again, hands shoulder width apart, and palms facing. Move your head back into its original position.

26

12. Turn your palms now so that they are facing downwards and angled towards you. Slowly lower your arms, all the way down to your sides, imagining that the energy emitted from your palms is calming, and cleansing your mind and body. During this process, imagine energy flowing from your palms, through your body, down the inside of your legs, and out through the arches in your feet.

13. Return to the starting position described in steps 1 – 4.

14. If you choose, you can now repeat steps 5 – 13, or conclude the exercise. When you are ready, gently open your eyes and let your tongue move back to its natural position.

With practise, this simple Qi Gong exercise can bring you to a level +1 or even 0 on the performance arousal scale, preparing you for those performing situations that require a state of physical and mental stillness and calm.

Why it works

The Basic Horse-stance Standing Meditation can be practised twice per day, morning and evening. It can have the effect of calming the entire body and mind, and expelling any residual negative performance arousal by activating the Parasympathetic Nervous System. Because of this, Qi Gong can be particularly useful for helping you to feel focussed, calm, positive, at ease, and in The Zone in your performing situations.

27. Role Models and Role Play

Role Playing is a technique which when adopted, can quickly help you to obtain an ideal state of mind for your performing situations, allowing you to perform in The Zone.

What is Role Play?

In essence, Role Playing to gain control over performance arousal involves pretending that you are someone that you look up to – someone who has done it all before, done it with ease, and had massive success. When you Role Play, you simply imitate certain qualities of a performer who has achieved what you would like to achieve. Having a role model is of course an essential element of Role Play. If you don't already have one or several role models, you'll need to complete the next exercise!

115

26
27

27a. Exercise: Finding a role model

Role models need not only be performers in your particular field of expertise. You may be an actor and admire how a certain sports person achieves 'In Zone' performances time and time again. You can transfer this sports person's certainty, confidence, comfort, or poise to yourself and your own field of performance.

Who in your field of performance do you admire?
Which performers outside of your field of performance do you admire?

List 5 possible role models here that you can use to help you complete the following two exercises:

Role model 1:

_____

The quality/qualities I admire about this person: _____

_____

How this quality/these qualities can help me in my performances:

_____

_____

_____

Role model 2:

_____

The quality/qualities I admire about this person: _____

_____

How this quality/these qualities can help me in my performances:

_____

_____

_____

Role model 3:

_____

The quality/qualities I admire about this person: _____

_____

How this quality/these qualities can help me in my performances: **117**

_____

_____

_____

Role model 4:

_____

The quality/qualities I admire about this person: _____

_____

How this quality/these qualities can help me in my performances: _____

_____

_____

_____

Role model 5:

_____

27

The quality/qualities I admire about this person: _____

_____

How this quality/these qualities can help me in my performances: _____

_____

_____

_____

27b. Exercise: Playing a Role in Non-Performing Situations

Although Role Playing probably comes naturally for the majority of actors and opera singers, it might not always seem quite so easy for those of us who consider ourselves less dramatically inclined.

One way to train Role Play for performance situations is to practise it in everyday situations.

Ask yourself the following: How would some of my role models act in my non-performing, day to day situations? What would they do and how would they do it?

You can ask yourself these questions and act out your answers in any situation, from simply walking down the street, to grocery shopping, to spending a night out on the town.

Study your role models and then spend perhaps just a few minutes of each day 'being' them. When it begins to feel that you can comfortably step into the character of a role model, you may like to try Role Playing in a training, rehearsal, or performance situation.

27c. Exercise: Playing a Role in Performing Situations

By regularly seeing your role models in action in their performing arena (the internet can be a great source of information here), you can get a great deal of inspiration about how to better tackle your own performing situations.

For example, if you find yourself feeling uneasy or anxious before your first photo shoot, one way to help you get closer to The Zone is to 'become' Claudia Schiffer. How would she handle the situation?

119

What about that next concert appearance? Why not 'become' Christina Aguilera? How would she perform in your situation?

On the way to your next casting audition, try 'becoming' Tom Hanks. What sort of impression would he make?

And before your next snooker tournament, 'become' Steve Davis. How would he appear if he was facing your opponent?

Use these templates to record your responses when Role Playing in performing situations:

Performing Situation: ⎯⎯⎯⎯⎯⎯⎯⎯⎯⎯⎯⎯⎯⎯⎯⎯⎯⎯⎯⎯⎯⎯⎯⎯

Role Model used: ⎯⎯⎯⎯⎯⎯⎯⎯⎯⎯⎯⎯⎯⎯⎯⎯⎯⎯⎯⎯⎯⎯⎯⎯⎯

How Role Playing this person helped me in my performance:

⎯⎯⎯⎯⎯⎯⎯⎯⎯⎯⎯⎯⎯⎯⎯⎯⎯⎯⎯⎯⎯⎯⎯⎯⎯⎯⎯⎯⎯⎯⎯⎯⎯⎯

⎯⎯⎯⎯⎯⎯⎯⎯⎯⎯⎯⎯⎯⎯⎯⎯⎯⎯⎯⎯⎯⎯⎯⎯⎯⎯⎯⎯⎯⎯⎯⎯⎯⎯

27

⎯⎯⎯⎯⎯⎯⎯⎯⎯⎯⎯⎯⎯⎯⎯⎯⎯⎯⎯⎯⎯⎯⎯⎯⎯⎯⎯⎯⎯⎯⎯⎯⎯⎯

Performing Situation: _____

Role Model used: _____

How Role Playing this person helped me in my performance:

_____

_____

_____

Performing Situation: _____

Role Model used: _____

How Role Playing this person helped me in my performance:

_____

_____

_____

The name of your chosen role model or simply the words "Role Play" or "role model" can also be written on a Cue Card to help remind you to use this technique.

Role Playing can be an extremely liberating and thoroughly enjoyable experience. Have some fun with this technique – there are a lot of possibilities here!

28. Self Talk: Angels and devils

No, this chapter isn't as biblical as it may sound! Do you remember those old cartoons, where sometimes a little angel would appear on one shoulder of the cartoon character, and a little devil would appear on the other? The little devil would say something like, "Go on, you know you want to!" and the angel would reply, "Don't do it, you know you shouldn't!" Then the devil would proceed to prod the angel with his trident, and the cartoon character would tip the bucket of water over the other person's head anyway.

Internal chatter

Just like in those old cartoons, our minds have the ability to create a constant chain of chatter in the form of words and images. Simplified, these words and images can be categorised as positive and constructive, or negative and destructive. One way to think about the different types of chatter that can happen in your mind is the way this chatter was depicted in those old cartoons – that is, spoken by a little angel and a little devil.

Which one do you listen to?

The little angel in your head (or on one shoulder) often says things such as, "You can do this. You're worthy. You deserve this." The little devil on the other hand (or shoulder), often with a much louder voice and bearing a freshly sharpened trident screams things like, "What happens if you screw up?! What will the other people think of you?! Maybe they don't like you?! OH MY GOD the sky is about to fall in on your head right now....oh, no, I mean now...no, now – it's going to happen to you!! Watch out! You're a loser and you are going to suck out there! You will fail!! What if it doesn't work!? You can't do it!! Panic!!"

Whew!

So, if you're in a position where your little angel is being tramped upon by a little devil shouting down a bull-horn, it's obvious what to do isn't it? Listen to the angel – he or she is in there somewhere. At the same time, you must learn to ignore the little devil – he or she is also there, and may never completely go away, but that doesn't mean you don't have to believe what he/she is saying.

So how do you concentrate on listening to the angel and believing your positive self talk, and ignoring the negative inner dialog? There are several ways to do this, but the exercise below is a fun one that can be adopted quickly and easily.

28. Exercise: Send him (or her) packing!

Firstly, give a name to the little devil. Think of something silly – something ridiculous. For this example I'm going to call him Dilly the devil – yes, Dilly.

Before, and during performing situations when Dilly starts making his presence felt by saying things like, "You might not make it! What happens if you screw up? What are all of those people going to think? How bad is this going to look for you!?" and so on, all you need to do is acknowledge Dilly's presence, and mentally tell him to go away, because you're busy at the moment with something more important.

So you might say to him, "I recognise that voice... Oh, it's you again. I'm busy with something else right now. Talk to you later Dilly. Bye!"

And then imagine Dilly gradually fading away into the distance.

A variation

As a variation on this technique, you might want to put a vivid mental image to Dilly. You may make Dilly look like a real person – perhaps someone from your past or present. Or, Dilly could be an imagined cartoon figure. Dilly the devil may also of course be male or female!

Imagine him/her talking to you with a silly hat on, or with one green sock, a wooden leg, or something even more ridiculous. Remember to acknowledge him/her, and then gently send him/her on his/her way, seeing him/her gradually fade away.

This technique of acknowledging and allowing your negative self-talk to fade away is another way of silencing the ego, allowing you easier access to optimal performance and The Zone.

This technique is also a prime candidate for inclusion on a Cue Card.

29. Self Talk: Think in the Positive

"Don't think of the colour red, don't think of the colour red, don't think of the colour red! Don't think RED!"

Pickle juice

What's the first thing you think of? You can be guaranteed that very few people, having read or heard the phrase "Don't think of the colour red!" think of the colour green, yellow, or something completely different such as pickle juice!

Not

The subconscious mind doesn't register the word "not", or phrases in the negative. Therefore repeating a phrase such as "Don't screw up, don't screw up, don't screw up!" is understood by the subconscious as "Screw up, screw up, screw up!" A powerful command that the subconscious knows very well how to implement.
We sometimes hear the phrases "Remove the negative" or "Don't think negatively!" These phrases in themselves are negatively charged and not particularly conducive to constructive thought patterns!

Reformulating

We must re-formulate these sentences, just as many of us must re-formulate our own self-talk. For example: "Don't think negatively" can be replaced with "Think in the positive." "Don't screw up" can be replaced with "I'm going to have a great performance!" The meaning behind these phrases is of course the same, however the results, as we've seen by how the subconscious treats the word not, are vastly different!
By becoming aware of, and formulating our inner dialogue in the positive, we can have a tremendous effect on how we perceive, and are perceived by the outer world. In your day to day life, the message is simple: Think and speak in the positive, and do it with true conviction! By doing this, you can help yourself to achieve a positive level of performance arousal in your performing situations.

30. Stay Away From Negative People

Throughout the history of the study of human psychology, the argument of 'Nature vs. Nurture' has been examined from many angles. Are our personalities the way they are because of genetics – nature? Or are our personalities the result of learned responses, established in early childhood and in constant change and/or reinforcement as we become older – nurture? Common thinking now is that both nature and nurture play a part, however our learned responses – nurture – seem to have a greater responsibility for the building of our personalities.

Shaping your personality

As the nurture side of the equation suggests, your personality can be shaped, modified, and reinforced by your interactions with the people around you. Therefore, who you associate with has a large bearing on who you are, how you feel, and of course, how you perform.

The good...

Imagine for a second that for your entire life you had only associated with positive people who look for solutions, appreciate what they have in life, strive to succeed and improve themselves and their lives on a consistent basis, and encourage and support you in anything you may wish to do. What sort of impact would these positive people have on you, your life, and your achievements? Do you think that these positive people would be able to help you succeed?

...and the bad

Now imagine the opposite for a minute if you will – a life spent associating with people who are masters at finding problems. People who can't find anything positive in life, who never even attempt to succeed and improve themselves because they 'know' they will fail, and worse still, tell you that you can't do it either in an attempt to bring you down to their level. They tell you that it's too difficult, too expensive, it takes too much time, and that there's no way you can succeed, so why bother trying? What sort of impact would these negative people have on you, your life, and your achievements? Do you think that these negative people would be able to help you succeed?

Avoiding negative people, and gravitating towards and associating with positive people can help you to achieve your full performing potential, and give you a greater chance of reaching The Zone in your field of performance.

Chapter 30

Becoming aware

As human beings we have an amazing capacity to adapt. We also have the property of being affected by the people around us. Look at the people around you and the relationships in your life. Which of the people in your life support you? Which people are 'blood-suckers', or 'energy-draining vampires'? Which people in your life encourage you? Which people discourage you? Which people in your life learn from their failures and aim for success? Which people wallow in their failures? When you have left or finished talking to certain people, do you feel better or worse?

Front row seats

It is important to realise that not everybody deserves a front row seat in your life. Do the current people in the front row seats of your life reflect who you are, or who you aspire to become? Do some people in your life need to take a seat further back, or even be shown the door? Do certain people deserve seats nearer the front? The point here is to never settle for second best (and certainly not third or fourth best) when it comes to the people you decide to have around you in your life. You deserve the very best. You are worth it!

By choosing to associate with positive, encouraging, and supportive people, and at the same time deciding to stay away from negative people, you can further help yourself to succeed in your journey to optimal performance.

30

31. Visualisation

Visualisation is a technique which can be employed to help 'program' your subconscious mind for success. When visualising, you use your imagination to see, hear, feel, and fully experience the results you would like to achieve.

The effects - a study in basketball

Several studies proving the effectiveness of visualisation have been carried out in the field of sports psychology. One such study involved the members of three basketball teams of approximately equal skill level, practising shooting '3-pointers', for a period of 30 days. One of the teams practised neither physically on the court, nor in their minds during the duration of the study. Their improvement at the end of the study was not surprisingly 0%. Another team practised physically – that is, on the basketball court – for a period of one hour each day. After 30 days, their improvement was measured at 24%. The third team did not practise physically at all but was told to mentally visualise the game for one hour each day. At the end of the thirty day period, their improvement was a remarkable 23%. But what was the reason for this?

The subconscious

Sports scientists concluded that the subconscious mind cannot differentiate between what is real and what is imagined. Since the subconscious mind exerts an immense amount of control over how we perform, visualisation practise can therefore have a large bearing on our success as performers.

Visualising in The Zone

For the purposes of *Performing in The Zone,* there are three specific types of visualisation techniques which will be explained here: Snap Shot, Intense Positive Visualisation, and the 5 Sense Visualisation method. With all visualisation techniques it is important to concentrate on the ideal. That is: What do you want to happen? What do you want to achieve? How do you want to feel? What would be the most fantastic, amazing, successful, effortless result possible? You must visualise yourself easily achieving your goal and having a great time doing it. You must concentrate on what you want and nothing else.

Different points of view

All visualisations can be carried out in the 1st person or 3rd person perspective. Using the 1st person perspective, you put yourself in the centre of the visualisation. For example, if you are a runway model, you may visualise yourself walking up and down the catwalk from your own eyes, taking in the experience as if you were actually carrying it out in reality.

In the 3rd person, you would see yourself from a distance, possibly from a seat in the audience, the back of the room, or even a position up in the ceiling somewhere above, behind, or beside you. Some performers find a 1st person visualisation to be more powerful and real, whereas others may find a 3rd person visualisation to be most effective. Experiment using both viewpoints in the following exercises, and discover which one works best for you.

Snap Shot

This is the simplest form of visualisation technique and one which can be practised anywhere at anytime. It takes literally a few seconds to complete, and can be very effective if used regularly throughout the day. The Snap Shot can even be executed with your eyes open, although with closed eyes the results can be considerably more effective.

Firstly, make clear in your mind what you want to achieve, and imagine yourself there actually in the situation – remember you can choose to see yourself from the outside as an observer – from the 3rd person perspective – or see the situation through your own eyes from the inside – the 1st person perspective. Try both and adopt the one that works best for you.

Now, you are about to create a mental image – a Snap Shot – of this fantastic, amazing, rewarding, effortless, "YES!", situation and feeling either before, during, or just as you complete your successful performance.

Create this image in your mind in as much detail as possible: Where are you? What does this location look like? What are you wearing? How are you standing or sitting? Are there stage lights? Camera flashes? What are you about to do, what are you doing, or what did you just do or achieve? How fantastic/amazing/rewarding does it feel?

Did you get your image?

Make this image as vibrant as possible. Once you have created your perfect Snap Shot image in your mind, you can of course take it with you wherever you go. Have it always at the ready, to be called upon whenever you choose to during the day. Start by 'looking' at your Snap Shot for a few seconds just 3 times per day. Because this visualisation exercise is so simple and can provide a lot of satisfaction, enjoyment, and yield rewarding results, you may find you want to consult your Snap Shot many times during the course of the day – and that's great!

31

To remind yourself to keep checking back at your Snap Shot, write a note to yourself and put it in a prominent place. Alternatively you can carry a Cue Card around with you. The Snap Shot visualisation exercise gently reminds your subconscious of where it is you that want to be – achieving optimal performance in The Zone.

Intense Positive Visualisation

For this technique, you will need to be undisturbed for a period of anywhere from ten minutes to an hour, depending on the length of the performance you are about to visualise.

Preparations

Intense Positive Visualisation is best carried out lying down on your back with your hands resting gently on your solar-plexus – I prefer lying flat on the floor or at times using a yoga mattress. Lying down on a bed can be an acceptable alternative, and is at times preferable if practising this exercise just before sleeping. It's important to keep the body at a comfortable temperature throughout the duration of the visualisation, and therefore covering yourself with a blanket might be necessary.

To begin, gently close your eyes, and lightly touch your tongue to the front part of the roof of your mouth, just behind the teeth. This is a Qi Gong technique which forms an energy bridge to allow freer flow of energy in the human energy system. Try to keep the root of your tongue relaxed at all times. If you have trouble with this, simply let your tongue sit in its natural position and come back to this Qi Gong energy bridge technique at a later stage.

Whilst in this horizontal position, allow the floor to take your weight. Feel your limbs becoming heavier the more relaxed they feel. Trust the floor – it will hold you. Give in to the support from underneath. Trust, relax, and let go. Breathe gently through your nose. Allow your body to breathe as it needs to.

The next section is designed to help you understand how Intense Positive Visualisation works. It is an example of one possible visualisation, taken from the perspective of a musician giving a recital, requiring a performance arousal level of +1 before the performance, +2 for the majority of the recital, and +3 for the climax of the concert. After reading and understanding this process, you can then create your own visualisation for your own specific needs. During your visualisation remember to visualise events exactly as you want them to be.

A Visualisation example

You begin by imagining yourself at home, taking your performance clothes out of the wardrobe. You check to see that everything is in order with your clothes and your performance shoes. You put your performance clothes and shoes in a suit bag, pick up your instrument case, check to see if you have your keys and wallet, and leave the house, locking the door behind you. You walk down the stairs and out on to the street in a relaxed pace. Arriving at the metro (underground train/'tube') station, you use your ticket to pass the barrier, and board your train. It's going to be a great show. Your performance arousal level is at +1. You feel relaxed, positive, and calm.

Getting off at the right stop, you stroll towards the recital hall, taking in the scenery on the way. Perhaps a seagull is calling in the distance? How do the trees look? Are there other people out walking? You take out your Cue Card and slowly read over your key words. Your performance arousal level is at +1. You feel relaxed, positive, and calm.

You arrive at the venue and greet the receptionist on the way in. After signing in, you head to your warm up room where your accompanist is already waiting for you. You ask your accompanist for 15 minutes by yourself so that you can prepare yourself and warm up. You unpack your instrument, and begin your warm up routine.

It feels fantastic to start warming up. You know your accompanist is going help you put on a great show. You know that the venue has a warm acoustic. Your performance clothes are ironed and your shoes polished. You are ready. You are about to share part of yourself with some people who want to hear you – they want to be touched by you. It's going to be a warm, giving, rewarding experience for both them and you. It's going to be great! Your performance arousal level is at +1. You feel relaxed, positive, and calm.

After 15 minutes your accompanist walks in to the room. Before you begin to rehearse, you check your Cue Card again, and go through your Pre-Performance Ritual, C3 – calm, controlled, confident – the C3 and "+1" on your Cue Card gives you a familiar, friendly reminder. You rehearse the beginning of the first piece with your accompanist. It's easy and free.

The acoustic in the practise room is dry, but you know that out there in the hall the space will take care of you – the warm reverb will beautify every nuance and add to the experience for everyone. Your performance arousal level is at +1. You feel relaxed, positive, and calm.

When it is time, you are called to the wings of the stage. You take one final look at your Cue Card and go through the C3 exercise again. You can hear the chatter of the audience, and see

31

the stage in front of you. You walk calmly, securely, and with purpose on to the stage where you are greeted by applause. They like you and you haven't even done anything yet! This is going to be a fun performance! Your performance arousal level is at +1. You feel relaxed, positive, and calm.

Whilst your accompanist adjusts the piano stool, you look out into the audience and make visual contact with the people you are about to touch with your performance. Your body language exudes confidence and assuredness. You greet the audience, introducing yourself and your accompanist and begin to talk about the evening's programme. Your voice is stable, powerful, and reflects the perfect +1 state of performance arousal that you are currently in. Your voice resonates effortlessly to the back of the hall. You are in The Zone.

After your brief introductory talk, you look to your accompanist who is ready to work with you. This is going great! You begin your performance, and your performance arousal gently rises to a +2.

At this point in the visualisation I strongly suggest that you visualise your entire performance – that is, see and hear yourself giving the most musical, fantastic, controlled, inspired, moving performance you can possibly imagine. Use either 1st or 3rd person perspective. In your visualisation you are doing everything right – it feels fantastic and sounds amazing. You are at an ideal level of performance arousal for this performing situation, and totally in The Zone.

Just before the climax of the final piece, you turn the page, and see the familiar figure of "+3" that you wrote earlier at the top of your music. You step it up a notch, and raise your performance arousal level to +3. The music takes on a new life and energy and this is felt by you, your accompanist, and the audience. Finishing the concert at a +3 level your audience erupts in cheers and applause. You did it! It was great!! You were in The Zone!!! You acknowledge the audience, and walk off stage.

When you feel ready, slowly begin to move your body again. How did it feel to give that amazing performance? You were great! Everything just 'clicked'. You were totally and completely in The Zone throughout the entire process.

Conscious practise becomes subconscious habit

Intense Positive Visualisation can be practised consciously every day before a performance. By doing so, you allow the habit of performing in The Zone to become subconscious. This type of visualisation is highly recommended to all performers about to give important performances, auditions or recitals. The earlier you begin Intense Positive Visualisation the better, but at least one week prior to the performance event should be the minimum.

Visualising an ideal level of performance arousal is important!

In your visualisations, remember to assess how much positive performance arousal you need at various moments: +1, +2, +3, +4, or +5. Do you need to be at the same activation level for the entire event, or does your performance arousal level need to modulate at various times? Remember that imagining yourself calm and relaxed probably isn't going to give you the best results if you are preparing for a +5 situation, such as in the professional wrestling example earlier. Likewise, visualising getting yourself psyched up and exploding out of the gates isn't going to help you if you are preparing for a more delicate +1 situation, such as the public chess championship.

131

Familiarity

By using Intense Positive Visualisation, you become familiar with as many elements of your performance day as possible, and become used to experiencing these always in a positive light. Notice also that Intense Positive Visualisation goes into as much detail as possible, both before and during your performance. This is to help take away as many surprises and unknown factors on the day of your performance as possible.

Reconnaissance and variation

It may help the accuracy and intensity of your visualisation to do some reconnaissance by actually visiting the performance venue prior to your performance event. This is easily possible for students giving final recitals for example, or sportspeople playing at a local venue.

Try to also incorporate some variations in your visualisations. Perhaps the audience isn't ready and takes an extra 5 minutes to get seated? Perhaps your accompanist arrives later than expected due to traffic problems? Maybe the stage curtains are blue and not red? Perhaps the warm up room is bigger or smaller?

Regardless of what happens, you are prepared, and you stay in your ideal level of positive performance arousal. You are completely stable, and in The Zone, always.

31

Getting the hang of it

By using Intense Positive Visualisation every day over a period of one week, you have in effect carried out your performance successfully 7 times. Practise this visualisation 3 times per day for a week and you've completed 21 successful, positive, great, fantastic, easy, ideal performances, and have been in The Zone every single time! Remember that your subconscious doesn't differentiate between what is real and what is imagined. Therefore by using Intense Positive Visualisation diligently, you are programming yourself for success by becoming familiar with performing in The Zone!

5 Sense Visualisation

This technique is an extension of Intense Positive Visualisation. However instead of only using your visual and aural senses, such as the musician's recital example, you now incorporate all 5 senses in your visualisation, if possible. This creates an even greater sense of realism which further increases the effect of the time spent visualising.

The senses

For example, when going through your visualisation, think about the physical sensations you feel before and during your performance. What sensations are you likely to feel in your body (or what physical sensations do you want to feel) before and during your performance? What are all of the sounds you are likely to hear (or what are the sounds that you want to hear) before and during your performance? What are you likely to see (or what is it that you want to see) before and during your performance? Are there likely to be any special smells or fragrances before or during your performance? Are there likely to be any special tastes in your mouth or flavours before or during your performance?

Visualisation - Conclusion

It cannot be emphasised enough that in all visualisations, an ideal level of positive performance arousal and a flawless performance should be strived for. In visualising, whether it be using the Snap Shot technique, Intense Positive Visualisation, or 5 Sense Visualisation, you are in a sense programming yourself – therefore the quality, intensity, accuracy, and ideal feeling or performance arousal level in your visualisations is paramount.

Remember the analogy of your brain working as a computer? By using these visualisation techniques to 'program' yourself for success, you are giving your mind "quality input" and therefore allowing yourself to experience "quality output." By visualising, you become more familiar with performing, and more used to obtaining an ideal level of performance arousal in your performing situations, allowing you to perform in The Zone.

32. Voice Quality

Closely related to body language, posture, and movement, the quality and resonance of your voice is a direct reflection of the state of your conscious and subconscious mind.

Your voice and state of mind

It is possible for you to learn a lot about yourself and current state of mind just by analysing the quality of your own voice. For example, when relaxed and calm, your voice may tend to have a deeper overall pitch, resonating without inhibitions of extraneous muscular tension. You may also notice that when you are relaxed you might have a tendency to speak more slowly than when excited, or anxious. Often, the more excited or anxious you are, the faster, more strained, more highly pitched your voice may become.

133

The body/mind connection

A distinct inter-relationship exists between your body and mind. That is to say that your mental state can alter your physical state, just as your physical state can alter your mental state. In regards to the voice, both chronic and acute anxiety or over-excitement can cause tension in the many muscles involved in voice production. However by consciously removing excess tension from muscles involved in speech, it is possible to remove excess excitement, tension, anxieties and the like, from the mind. Removing this excess vocal tension can have a powerful impact on how your performance arousal is manifested.

31
32

32a. Exercise: How does your voice sound?

If you suffer from anxiety or over-excitement in performing or everyday situations, you may be able to resolve this by examining and changing the way you use your voice.

Read the previous sentence again, although this time out loud, and in your normal speaking voice. You may even wish to listen to a recording of yourself speaking. Once you have done this, use a pen or pencil to mark your answers along the lines in the figure below:

My normal speaking voice tends to be . . .

EXAMPLE:

low-pitched ————————— X ————————— high-pitched

relaxed ————————— X ————— tense

slow ————————————— X — fast

full and resonant ————————— X ————— thin and scratchy

never hoarse — X ——————————————— always hoarse

low-pitched ————————————————— high-pitched

relaxed ————————————————— tense

slow ————————————————— fast

full and resonant ————————————————— thin and scratchy

never hoarse ————————————————— always hoarse

If you find that one or more of your markers tends heavily towards the right hand side of the lines, and that you regularly feel anxious or over-excited in performing or everyday situations, changing the way you use your voice may be of benefit to you.

Here are some tips for using your voice to reduce both anxiety and excessive excitement:

- Allow the pitch of your voice to drop to its natural level
- Relax the muscles around your hips, shoulders and neck when speaking
- Speak slowly, and be comfortable with silence
- Allow yourself and your voice to take space
- Reduce excess tension in your face, tongue, and jaw when speaking
- Imagine that your entire body resonates when you speak, not just your larynx (voice box)
- Learn more about how to use your voice from a qualified vocal/speech instructor

In addition, you may also like to try the following exercise to help you explore and experience how your voice can affect your state of mind.

32b. Exercise: Explore your voice

Find a location where you know you won't be disturbed. Make sure this is a place where you can feel completely uninhibited to experiment with your voice. Take an assortment of written material with you. Children's stories can be ideal for this exercise.

To begin with, read your texts aloud, and in front of a mirror if possible. Become completely immersed in the story or text that you are reading. 'Sell' the text as if you believe in it 100%! Remember that no one can see or hear you! Therefore, it doesn't matter if you think you appear or sound foolish during this exercise. Turn off your ego and have some fun!

After having read several passages being completely immersed in the text, go on to explore a variety of emotions and moods whilst reading aloud. How does your voice sound, and how does it affect your state of mind when you express total happiness, deep sorrow, carefree glee, utter boredom, maximum stress, complete calm, and so on. Vary the tone and pitch of your voice, volume, and even accent or dialect.

Think about an ideal state of mind for your performing situations. Can you express this state of mind in your voice when reading your text?

How does your voice sound, what facial expression or expressions do you show, and how do you use your body when you are reflecting an ideal amount of performance arousal for your performing situations? Can you adopt this voice, facial expression or expressions, and body language in your daily life?

Experimenting with your own voice can be a powerful means of breaking habitual anxieties or excessive excitement in everyday situations. By getting used to living daily life in The Zone through the power of your voice, your state of mind in performing situations can also improve.

33. Conclusion – Five Favourites

Now that you've had a chance to read through and experiment with the tools and techniques in Part Two, it's time for one final exercise before moving on to Part Three: The Programme.

33. Exercise: Five Favourites

List your 5 favourite techniques/exercises from Part Two:

Favourite technique/exercise #1 _____

Situation where I used this: _____

How this technique/exercise helped me: _____

_____

_____

_____

_____

_____

Favourite technique/exercise #2 _____

Situation where I used this: _____

How this technique/exercise helped me: _____

_____

_____

_____

_____

32
33

Favourite technique/exercise #3 _____

Situation where I used this: _____

How this technique/exercise helped me: _____

_____

_____

_____

_____

_____

Favourite technique/exercise #4 _____

Situation where I used this: _____

How this technique/exercise helped me: _____

_____

_____

_____

_____

_____

Favourite technique/exercise #5 _____

Situation where I used this: _____

How this technique/exercise helped me: _____

_____

_____

_____

_____

_____

PART THREE
The Programme

34
wk 1
wk 2
wk 3
wk 4
wk 5
wk 6
wk 7
wk 8
wk 9
wk 10
wk 11
wk 12
35
36

34. The 12 Week Performance Success Programme

It is doubtful that simply understanding the ideas presented in Part One of this book, and only reading about the techniques in Part Two will help you to any great extent in reaching The Zone in your field of performance. It is for this reason that you've been encouraged to complete the many exercises that have been included so far in this book, and experiment with the techniques in Part Two. In this way you become an active participant in your own development towards controlled performance arousal and optimum performance.

Have you put pen (or pencil) to paper and completed the exercises? Have you had the opportunity to experiment with some of the techniques from Part Two? Which were your five favourites?

The 4 Step Success Strategy

One way now to speed your progress to optimal performance – being in The Zone state of mind – is to follow the effective and efficient 4 Step Success Strategy outlined below:

Step 1

Understand what The Zone is. Know about performance arousal.
Read about the techniques in Part Two of this book.

Step 2

Have a plan for incorporating the techniques into your performing life and then follow through by actually incorporating the techniques into your performing life.

Step 3

Assess which techniques work for you and which don't.

Step 4

If necessary, go back to Step 2, modifying your plan based on your assessment in Step 3.

If you have read about the theory of performance arousal in Part One, know what The Zone is, and have also read through the various techniques outlined in Part Two, then congratulations – you've completed Step 1! It is now time to move to Step 2.

Have a plan

Step 2 is to use The 12 Week Performance Success Programme as your plan for incorporating the techniques in the preceding chapters into your performing life, and then follow through by actually incorporating the techniques into your performing life! This is the most challenging and most rewarding part of the process. By taking this second step, you are implementing the knowledge you have gained from what you have already read, and applying it to your own real life situations.

Give yourself a chance

Do not just sit there thinking to yourself "Yeah, I guess this stuff would work", or, "I'm not really sure about all of this", and then put this book back on your bookshelf after you've finished reading it! Be fair on yourself. Give yourself this chance to make a change in your performing life. Follow through with The 12 Week Performance Success Programme from beginning to end, at least once. You are the master of your performing life and the master of yourself. By taking action using The 12 Week Performance Success Programme in this part of *Performing in The Zone*, you too can master your performance arousal level and achieve optimum performance.

What, Why and How

To give yourself the best possible chance of success, you must ask yourself all of the questions from the 'What, Why and How' exercise in Chapter 5. If you haven't completed this exercise yet, do it **right now**. If you have completed the exercise, read through your answers again. Do this now, and then come back to this page!

Motivation

If you ever find yourself lacking motivation at any time over the coming 12 weeks, re-reading your answers to the questions in Chapter 5 may help to spur you on. Another way to help with motivation throughout The 12 Week Performance Success Programme is to go through the programme with a fellow performer, and support each other when necessary.

The programme

The 12 Week Performance Success Programme has been specifically designed to get you performing in The Zone as quickly and efficiently as possible. The effects may be felt at any point during the course of the programme – in the lead-up to Week 12, in your final public or private performance at the end of Week 12, or perhaps, even at some time in the future.

When you have followed through The 12 Week Performance Success Programme from beginning to end, you will be able to complete Step 3 of the 4 Step Success Strategy – self assessment. By taking this step you will gain a clearer understanding of the techniques that work best for you.

You can then take Step 4, and go back to the beginning of The 12 Week Performance Success Programme revising and reinventing it just for you, using your preferred techniques from this book, techniques from other sources, or a combination of both. In this way you are constantly improving and refining your own mental game, and getting ever closer to unleashing your true performing potential by performing in The Zone.

With the 4 Step Success Strategy, The 12 Week Performance Success Programme, the techniques and tools in Part 2 of this book, and your motivation gained from the 'What, Why and How' exercise in Chapter 5, you can get closer to performing in The Zone!

Building up

If you had attempted to lift the biggest and heaviest weights when you first began training at a gym, one of two things would probably have happened: The first is that you might have lifted the weight once, or even a couple of times, but then the pain and stiffness your body would have felt over the following days would have quickly told you, "Hey! Don't do that again!" The other possibility is of course that you wouldn't have managed to lift the weight at all, as it was simply too much to handle. Going to the gym for the first time and attempting the heaviest weights from the first day can be compared to attempting all of the techniques in this book at the same time. Even if it was possible for you to manage all of the techniques over a day or so, you would more than likely experience overwhelm – the net result being that you may go away disparaged and confused, possibly not having made any progress at all.

That is why The 12 Week Performance Success Programme is the best way to achieve success in finding The Zone quickly, efficiently, and systematically. This programme presents a plan which is manageable due to its bite-size, understandable, and achievable pieces. The 12 Week Performance Success Programme creates and gradually builds positive momentum, giving you the time to experiment, learn, stretch, relax, and consolidate – just as in any good weight training programme.

How and When to Start

An effective and simple approach to The 12 Week Performance Success Programme is to begin each week of training on a Monday, and work through to Friday, taking the weekends off. However you may choose to follow The 12 Week Performance Success Programme for 6 or even a full 7 days per week, depending on your personal training/practise schedule. For the purposes of The 12 Week Performance Success Programme, it is ideal if you can set aside a full 11 weeks where you have no actual performances scheduled, and then either:

a) Have a public performance scheduled for the end of week 12 or
b) Schedule a private performance for friends/family/colleagues for the end of week 12

If setting aside a full 11 weeks without performances is impossible for you in your current situation, don't worry. Use this programme, and work towards a specific public or private performance in Week 12 anyway!

Following through

You may wish to read through the entire The 12 Week Performance Success Programme before beginning to use it. That is fine! However be sure that when you have finished reading through The 12 Week Performance Success Programme, you go back to Week 1 and begin to **implement the programme!** Once you start the 12 Week Performance Success Programme, follow it through to the end, and judge the results for yourself. Most importantly, **have fun** with it! Let's begin!

Week 1: Getting started

I am what I eat. I am what I think.

Goals for this week:

- Create structure in your daily and weekly routine
- Make dietary changes if necessary
- Make exercise changes if necessary
- Implement these changes for the duration of this programme and **make them habits**

In Week 1, the focus is on your physical body and health, as well as how you make use of that precious commodity – time.

Disclaimer: The information given below is in no way intended to replace specialist medical advice provided by a health professional. Should you suspect that you have a health problem you should visit a health professional immediately.

Diet

For a moment let's think about a high-performance car. The car is made up of a lot of individual parts. If one of these parts isn't functioning as it should, the car's performance is negatively affected – it is unable to perform to its optimal level.

Your engine

Your body is also made up of many different parts – bones, fluids, muscles, tendons, and a whole host of organs – each with a particular job to do. The engine in a high-performance car requires fuel, oxygen, and a spark in order for it to work. Your 'engine' is exactly the same. You receive fuel in the form of food and water, and oxygen from the air you breathe. Instead of spark-plugs to ignite the fuel, you have digestive enzymes which allow food energy and nutrients to be assimilated and transported to various parts of your system.

Different types of engines and fuels

What would happen if you put the wrong type of fuel, such as cooking oil, in a high-performance, petrol driven car? Would the performance of the car be affected? Yes! The car's engine would not be able to run smoothly – that is, if it was even able to start at all!

As humans, thanks to evolution our 'engines' (our digestive systems) have naturally adapted so that they can utilise a wide variety of 'fuels'. Certain 'engines' seem to run effectively on almost anything, whereas others react negatively to certain 'fuels' that they are provided with. Examples of these negative reactions can be allergies to particular foods, as well as intolerance to gluten and lactose. For you to achieve optimum physical and mental performance, and have the best chance of finding the ideal mind state for your performing situations, you need to understand your 'engine', and the types of 'fuels' you consume.

145

Which foods should you avoid?

How do you find out which types of foods are optimal for your body? A food allergy test can be performed by many health professionals, and can give you a basic understanding of which foods (if any) you should avoid. Other tests which can give important information on the functioning of your digestive system are tests for bacterial balance, as well as tests for various parasites. Such tests are generally carried out by specialised laboratories, and unfortunately tend not to be covered by state medical care. However, if you regularly experience problems with your digestive system, an appointment with a health professional or testing laboratory should be prioritised.

How you use your body also affects how your digestive system utilises the 'fuels' you consume. You must eat the right foods for your body and your type of physical activity. This will help both your body and mind to set up the best possible pre-requisites for performing in The Zone.

Common sense

Of course common sense also plays a large role here. For example, we all know, and this is now proven by various high-profile studies and documentaries, that excessive consumption of 'food' produced by the fast-food industry can be damaging to health. The negative physical and mental effects of smoking, recreational drugs, and the excessive consumption of alcohol are also well documented. Treat your body with the respect it deserves. After all, you only have one body, and no amount of money in the world, with today's technology at least, can replace it.

Eastern wisdom - Tao

According to Taoist health experts we should eat enzyme-rich foods. These are either fresh raw foods, or lightly cooked or steamed meals which have not had the nutrients burnt out of their individual ingredients. In addition, as our bodies are approximately 70% water, ingesting high water content foods can help us to maintain a stable fluid balance.

Many doctors of Traditional Chinese Medicine will also advise consuming warm foods, as the difference between the temperature of chilled foods and the temperature of the stomach can cause discomfort, gas, and a less effective assimilation of nutrients. And finally, an appropriate balance of acidic and alkaline foods is required for optimal digestive function. As many of the foods available today are considerably more acidic than alkaline, it can be worthwhile to discover where the pH balance of your regular diet lies, making changes as necessary.

Diet - Learning more

A complete discussion on the subject of nutrition is unfortunately outside the realms of this book. However, personalised information about nutrition as well as an ideal diet for your lifestyle can be obtained by qualified nutritionists. You may also choose to seek out the various resources found in the Bibliography and Suggested Further Reading section of this book, as well as consult Chapter 38: Diet and Exercise, to provide you with a more complete picture.

Exercise

How many times have you tried a new exercise regime? Perhaps purchased a year-long gym membership only to 'forget' about going after the 1st month because you became caught up with other things that were just 'too important'?

As a species we can be very adept at finding a lot of 'good' reasons not to be doing the things we know we should. That is why at times we have to be our own 'policemen' or 'minders'. By that I mean we have to enforce structure upon ourselves as a way of conditioning ourselves for success.

The Godfather of Fitness

Jack LaLanne, the 'Godfather of Fitness', who is physically active and still exercises for a full two hours every day without fail at age of 94 (at the date of writing) states, "Exercise is King, Nutrition is Queen. Put them together and you've got a kingdom." And of course the contrary of maintaining physical inactivity and a poor diet is the fastest route to disease and ultimately premature death.

You are made to move

One may even say that you are a moving machine. And just like any machine, if lack of movement prevails for too long, your hinges become rusty. Therefore, you need to activate yourself, and set aside a certain amount of time every day for physical movement – you may even want to call this...exercise! The word "exercise" does not need to incorporate the 'No pain, no gain' strategy. In fact you might even say that this attitude can be counter-productive! Instead, what you need to do is achieve a manageable, moderate, painless, and even enjoyable period of 'physical movement', preferably every day.

A gentle start

One way to achieve this is simply by getting out of the house each morning as soon as you wake up, and beginning the day by taking a brisk walk for approximately 30 minutes. You may increase the intensity by incorporating various stretches, lightly jogging, or even including some basic callisthenic and strength exercises.

If you already have a strict training programme incorporating diet and exercise in your weekly practise schedule, or are a dancer or athlete, you may at this stage choose to go directly to Week 2 of The 12 Week Performance Success Programme.

30 Minutes of Motion

For the purposes of The 12 Week Performance Success Programme, the best time of the day for you to exercise is the morning, but any time of day is acceptable – as long as you do it! Therefore, "30 Minutes of Motion" should be incorporated into your schedule and carried out every day for the rest of this 12 week programme, as this **gentle and regular physical activation is a key component to performing in The Zone.**

To help remind you to complete your daily 30 Minutes of Motion, you will need to create a schedule for yourself for the coming weeks, and stick to it. Revise Chapter 21 – My Time, and Intelligent Time Management.

So to recap, your assignments for this week:

1. Examine your diet and make changes if necessary – don't put junk in your engine!
2. Exercise – 30 Minutes of Motion every day – enjoy being alive – move and stretch!!
3. Make a schedule and stick to it. Incorporate 30 Minutes of Motion into your schedule.

Approximate time required: 30 – 60 minutes/day

Notes - Week 1:

_____

_____

_____

_____

_____

Week 2:   Letting go

I would like to do this.
I want to do this.
I should do this.
I must do this.
I am this.

Goals for this week:

- Continue with 30 Minutes of Motion every day
- Begin with Free Writing

This week, in addition to your daily 30 Minutes of Motion, you will need to set aside a period of 15 minutes for your next daily assignment – Free Writing. It is important that you can carry out this exercise undisturbed. Use the timetable that you created last week and schedule a time each day for your Free Writing session. Your 30 Minutes of Motion and Free Writing must be prioritised! Go back to Free Writing in Chapter 13 and read over the instructions and guidelines once more. Remember that there are no rules with Free Writing – you are free to write about anything you choose.

A helping hand

If you experience blocks or simply need some help to get you started, try writing a few words on the following topics:

- a previous or up-coming performance
- a list of the positive emotions you've felt over the past days (happy, excited etc) and what made you feel those emotions
- a list of the negative emotions you've felt over the past days (sad, worried, anxious etc) and ways you might alleviate these emotions
- positive internal and external qualities that you have which make you unique
- the things you are truly grateful for in your life

You may wish to go out today to purchase a hard-backed book with blank pages to use as your Free Writing journal, or you may simply choose to use any computer-based word processing package. Remember to date your entries. If a part of you is having trouble finding motivation to follow through with this exercise, simply read through your answers to the questions in Chapter 5 again. If necessary, do this now, and then come straight back to this page!

Your assignments for this week:

1. Exercise – 30 Minutes of Motion every day – enjoy being alive – move and stretch!!
2. Free Writing – 15 minutes, undisturbed

wk 2

Approximate time required: 45 minutes/day

Notes - Week 2:

149

Week 3: Snap Shot

Concentrating on solutions is the best way to solve problems.

Goals for this week:

- Continue with 30 Minutes of Motion every day
- Continue with Free Writing
- Create and make use of a Snap Shot

In addition to your daily 30 Minutes of Motion and 15 minutes of Free Writing, this week you will be implementing the first of the simple yet powerful visualisation techniques – Snap Shot visualisation.

Firstly, go back to Chapter 31 and revise this 'do-anywhere' technique. Once you have created your Snap Shot, begin to incorporate it at least 3 times at various stages throughout each day this week, and for the remainder of this programme.

Your assignments for this week:

1. Exercise – 30 Minutes of Motion every day – enjoy being alive – move and stretch!!
2. Free Writing – 15 minutes, undisturbed
3. Visualisation: Create a Snap Shot and use it at least 3 times per day.

Approximate time required: 50 – 60 minutes/day

Notes - Week 3:

Week 4:   Focus and flexibility

"When man is born, he is soft and supple;
When he dies, he is hard and rigid.
So it is with all things.
All plants and animals are soft in life,
But brittle and dry in death.
Therefore, to be hard and rigid is the way of death;
To be soft and supple is the way of life."

– Lao Tze, Tao Teh Ching, chapter 76.

Goals for the week:

- Continue with 30 Minutes of Motion every day
- Continue with 15 minutes of Free Writing
- Continue to make use of your Snap Shot
- Think about and create your own Mantra and other Pre-Performance Rituals
- Begin Qi Gong or Tai Chi for centring and focussing purposes

Now it's time to revise Chapter 25, Pre-Performance Rituals and Mantras. Spend some time thinking about and creating your own Mantra and other Pre-Performance Rituals. Remember, these tools are reminders to get you quickly into The Zone. Try to come up with at least 1 unique Mantra and 3 Pre-Performance Rituals which you can experiment with over the coming weeks. You can of course use the examples given in Chapter 25 if these work best for you and your performing situations.

Qi Gong and Tai Chi

In addition, using the words of Lao Tze as inspiration, you will be delving into the ancient Chinese soft-style martial art of Qi Gong. If possible, include two Qi Gong practise sessions each day – one in the morning and one in the evening. Remember to include this in your schedule! To begin with, you may use the Qi Gong instructions found in Chapter 26 of this book. However, for a more complete description of Qi Gong, and for further exercises, you can join a Qi Gong class, enlist the help of a qualified private teacher, or seek out the resources listed later in the section Bibliography and Suggested Further Reading.

As an alternative to Qi Gong, you may choose to practise Tai Chi. For the purposes of The 12 week Performance Success Programme, the benefits of Qi Gong and Tai Chi are similar.

Your assignments for this week:

1. Exercise – 30 Minutes of Motion every day – enjoy being alive – move and stretch!!
2. Free Writing – 15 minutes, undisturbed
3. Visualisation: Use your Snap Shot at least 3 times per day.
4. Create at least 1 Mantra and 3 Pre-Performance Rituals to experiment with.
5. Practise Qi Gong as described in this book or extend the exercise by attending a class or taking private lessons. Alternatively, practise Tai Chi. Practise preferably twice per day, for 15 minutes at a time

Approximate time required: 75 – 90 minutes/day

Notes - Week 4:

_____

_____

_____

_____

_____

_____

_____

_____

_____

_____

_____

_____

_____

_____

_____

_____

_____

Week 5:   Intense Positive Visualisation

You've got two options: Either you go out there and kick some a**,
or you wait here until your a** gets kicked – it's your call.

Goals for this week:

- Continue with 30 Minutes of Motion every day
- Continue with Free Writing
- Continue to make use of your Snap Shot
- Continue with Qi Gong or Tai Chi (if time permits)
- Begin Intense Positive Visualisation, using your Mantra and other Pre-Performance Rituals

Now that you are starting to get some routine, it is time to increase the intensity of the programme somewhat by incorporating the powerful 'subconscious programming' technique of Intense Positive Visualisation.

Time

At this point in time you may find that your daily schedule is filling up. Therefore, only if necessary, you may choose to omit one or both of your Qi Gong or Tai Chi practise sessions to make room for Intense Positive Visualisation. However, for best possible results I recommend that you endeavour to complete both of these exercises each day. Another option is to alternate your practise, devoting one day to Qi Gong or Tai Chi, and the next to Intense Positive Visualisation.

Intense Positive Visualisation, Mantras, and Pre-Performance Rituals

Revise Intense Positive Visualisation in Chapter 31. If appropriate for your field of performance, you can begin to incorporate your Mantra and other Pre-Performance Rituals into your Intense Positive Visualisation practise.

You can perhaps experiment by visualising a different Pre-Performance Ritual or Mantra each day. In this way you can become familiar with a number of Pre-Performance Rituals and Mantras, and be ready to incorporate these when you begin Practising Performing later in the programme.

Eventually you will have a small number of powerful Pre-Performance Rituals and a Mantra that you can access where ever and whenever you need them. These next few weeks are your chance for many 'dry runs'.

Gradually moving forward

We're gently adding more weights to the bar. If this is your first time through The 12

Week Performance Success Programme then remember that you don't need to be able to master all of the exercises right away. It may take you two or three repetitions of the entire programme before you feel completely comfortable with all of the exercises – and that is completely okay. Take as much time as you need. What is important is that you are heading in the right direction. Remember that moving gradually forward is much better than going full speed in reverse!

wk 5

Your assignments for this week:

1. Exercise – 30 Minutes of Motion every day – enjoy being alive – move and stretch!!
2. Free Writing – 15 minutes, undisturbed
3. Visualisation: Use your Snap Shot at least 3 times per day.
4a. Practise Qi Gong as described in this book, or extend the exercise by attending a class or taking private lessons. Alternatively, practise Tai Chi. Practise preferably twice per day, for 15 minutes at a time

and/or

4b. Begin Intense Positive Visualisation. Incorporate your Mantra and Pre-Performance Rituals from Week 4 of The 12 Week Performance Success Programme.

Approximate time required: 90 – 120 minutes/day

Notes - Week 5:

_____

_____

_____

_____

_____

_____

_____

_____

_____

_____

Week 6: Adding value

"What can I do to add value to my own life and the lives of others?"
— Nathan Schacherer

Goals for this week:

- Continue with 30 Minutes of Motion every day
- Continue with Free Writing
- Continue to make use of your Snap Shot
- Continue with Qi Gong or Tai Chi (if time permits)
- Continue with Intense Positive Visualisation, using your Mantra and other Pre-Performance Rituals
- Begin to Add Value

As a gentle addition to Week 5, this week you can concentrate on Adding Value – both to your own life as well as the lives of others. This can be done in any number of ways, and need not be a complex or time consuming process. The classic example of helping the old lady across the street is perhaps one of the most obvious ways of adding value to someone else's life.

The value of adding value

By seeking to add value to your own life, you can improve the quality and enjoyment of your life experience. By adding value to the lives of others, you are practising humility, silencing the ego, and thereby getting ever closer to The Zone. Revise Chapter 7 – Adding Value. Try to add value to your own life as well as at least one other person's life every day. You may soon find this so rewarding that you will be always looking for opportunities to Add Value.

Reminders

The simple assignment of Adding Value will most likely not take a great deal of time or energy, giving you the opportunity to further hone your Qi Gong or Tai Chi skills, as well as to further improve your Intense Positive Visualisation.

Remember when practising Qi Gong or Tai Chi to keep your movements relaxed and flowing. When visualising, keep your visualisations as vivid and accurate as possible, with an ideal level of positive performance arousal in mind. Have fun imagining giving the perfect performance!

Your assignments for this week:

1. Exercise – 30 Minutes of Motion every day – enjoy being alive – move and stretch!!
2. Free Writing – 15 minutes, undisturbed
3. Visualisation: Use your Snap Shot at least 3 times per day.
4a. Practise Qi Gong as described in this book, or extend the exercise by attending a class or taking private lessons. Alternatively, practise Tai Chi. Practise preferably twice per day, for 15 minutes at a time

and/or

4b. Practise Intense Positive Visualisation. Incorporate your Mantra and Pre-Performance Rituals from Week 4 of The 12 Week Performance Success Programme.
5. Add value to your life and the lives of others every single day

Approximate time required: 90 – 120 minutes/day

Notes - Week 6:

Week 7:   5 Sense Visualisation, and Silence

We must learn from the past, strive to be better tomorrow,
and at the same time be happy with who we are today, right now.

Goals for this week:

- Continue with 30 Minutes of Motion every day
- Continue with Free Writing
- Continue to make use of your Snap Shot
- Continue with Qi Gong or Tai Chi (if time permits)
- Continue to Add Value to your own life and the lives of others
- Begin 5 Sense Visualisation, using your Mantra and Pre-Performance Rituals
- Experiment with silence

Week 7 takes no drastic departure from Week 6. However, now it is time to increase the intensity and thereby effectiveness of Intense Positive Visualisation by using full 5 Sense Visualisation. This may require more concentration at first, but after a short time you will find yourself naturally 'seeing, hearing, touching', and where appropriate, 'smelling' or even 'tasting' the performance environment.

Incorporating all of the senses

These last two senses may at first not seem to be relevant in all performing situations, however they do occur. Field sports athletes for example are very used to the smell of fresh grass on a wet pitch, models are familiar with the dofts of various hair-sprays and other beauty products, and stage actors may be used to the sweet smell (and at times taste) of 'sugar smoke'. Remember that with 5 Sense Visualisation you are trying to involve all of your senses if possible, to create the most real visualisation possible. If you find it difficult to incorporate all 5 senses in your visualisation don't worry! The most important thing is that you attempt to make your visualisations as vivid and lifelike as possible.

Silence

This week you can also experiment with silence by adding the exercise 'Give it a rest!' into your schedule. Read up on this in Chapter 10 – Excessive Talk, and Silence. Try to set aside a certain period of the day where you can be silent. Remember to remain conscious and aware. Observe your surroundings, but don't comment, analyse, or pass judgement on them. Enjoy this state of silence, not uttering a single word, or communicating in any way for a full 15 minutes, or more. Remember also that a true silent state is a passive state, and therefore reading, writing emails, or watching T.V.

does not count as practising the art of silence! Enjoy the liberating reprieve of calming your external and internal chatter.

Your assignments for this week:

1. Exercise – 30 Minutes of Motion every day – enjoy being alive – move and stretch!!
2. Free Writing – 15 minutes, undisturbed
3. Visualisation: Use your Snap Shot at least 3 times per day.
4a. Practise Qi Gong as described in this book, or extend the exercise by attending a class or taking private lessons. Alternatively, practise Tai Chi. Practise preferably twice per day, for 15 minutes at a time

and/or

4b. Practise 5 Sense Visualisation. Incorporate your Mantra and Pre-Performance Rituals from Week 4 of The 12 Week Performance Success Programme.
5. Add value to your life and the lives of others every single day
6. Experiment with silence

Approximate time required: 120 – 150 minutes/day

Notes - Week 7:

_____

_____

_____

_____

_____

_____

_____

_____

_____

_____

_____

wk 7

Week 8: Practising Performing - Step 1

"Work smarter, not harder" – Trad.

Goals for this week:

- Continue with 30 Minutes of Motion every day
- Continue with Free Writing
- Continue to make use of your Snap Shot
- Continue with Qi Gong or Tai Chi (if time permits)
- Continue to Add Value to your own life and the lives of others
- Continue 5 Sense Visualisation, using your Mantra and Pre-Performance Rituals
- Continue to experiment with silence
- Begin Practising Performing – Step 1
- Experiment with Going Peripheral
- Create Cue Cards

Practising Performing – Step 1

We're up to week 8! Great! Are you sticking to the programme? I hope so because this is where the real fun starts! Over the past 7 weeks if you've followed the programme you will have established a secure base from which to proceed to the next step – Practising Performing! This week you need to review Practising Performing – 5 Steps to Mastery, in Chapter 24, and begin Step 1 – Practise Performing in your mind.

Going Peripheral

In addition, you may also include the tool of Going Peripheral as shown in Chapter 15. This technique may be practised separately before being incorporated when Practising Performing. For example you may choose to practise Going Peripheral on command in any situation throughout the course of a normal day.

Make a note of the effects of Going Peripheral. How do you feel before, and after Going Peripheral? How does it affect you in various situations? Experiment with this technique – is it a technique that could work for you?

Cue Cards

And finally, it's time now to start creating some Cue Cards to help remind you of the techniques you will be implementing over the coming weeks, as well as the level of positive performance arousal you want to achieve in your performing situations. Experiment with various Cue Cards over the coming weeks and keep those that work best for you. We're building up further and moving in the right direction! Chart your progress now in the Performance Journal in Appendix 2 (or use a blank book or computer), and enjoy the momentum!

Your assignments for this week:

1. Exercise – 30 Minutes of Motion every day – enjoy being alive – move and stretch!!
2. Free Writing – 15 minutes, undisturbed
3. Visualisation: Use your Snap Shot at least 3 times per day.
4a. Practise Qi Gong as described in this book or extend the exercise by attending a class or taking private lessons. Alternatively, practise Tai Chi. Practise preferably twice per day, for 15 minutes at a time

and/or

4b. Continue 5 Sense Visualisation, using your Pre-Performance Rituals
5. Add value to your life and the lives of others every single day
6. Continue experimenting with silence
7. Practise Performing – Step 1, using your Mantra and other Pre-Performance Rituals, and including the technique of Going Peripheral
8. Create and use Cue Cards
9. Make notes in your performance journal

Approximate time required: 90 – 180 minutes/day

Notes - Week 8:

Week 9:   Practising Performing - Step 2

"Embrace change – Nothing in life ever stays the same,
it either withers or it grows"

— John (Jack) Lauderdale

Goals for this week:

- Continue with 30 Minutes of Motion every day
- Continue with Free Writing
- Continue to make use of your Snap Shot
- Continue with Qi Gong or Tai Chi (if time permits)
- Continue to Add Value to your own life and the lives of others
- Continue 5 Sense Visualisation, using your Mantra and Pre-Performance Rituals
- Continue to experiment with silence
- Begin Practising Performing – Step 2
- Experiment with Going Peripheral and/or 'E=mc^2'
- Use Cue Cards

Practising Performing – Step 2

This week marks another big step towards your goal of performing in The Zone. During this week you are going to begin working with the second step of Practising Performing. Remember to review this step in Chapter 24.

More techniques

In addition to Step 2 of Practising Performing, you can continue to use the technique of Going Peripheral as well as begin to experiment with the technique of 'E=mc^2' as explained in Chapter 11. When Practising Performing, you can also incorporate your Mantra or any other Pre-Performance Rituals you may choose.

Which techniques seem to be working best for you? Remember to track your progress this week in your performance journal. Have fun!

Your assignments for this week:

1. Exercise – 30 Minutes of Motion every day – enjoy being alive – move and stretch!!
2. Free Writing – 15 minutes, undisturbed
3. Visualisation: Use your Snap Shot at least 3 times per day.
4a. Practise Qi Gong as described in this book or extend the exercise by attending a class or taking private lessons. Alternatively, practise Tai Chi. Practise preferably twice per day, for 15 minutes at a time

and/or

4b. Continue 5 Sense Visualisation, using your Pre-Performance Rituals and Mantra
5. Add value to your life and the lives of others every single day
6. Continue experimenting with silence
7. Practise Performing – Step 2 using your Mantra and other Pre-Performance Rituals, and including Going Peripheral and/or 'E=mc^2'
8. Use Cue Cards
9. Make notes in your performance journal

Approximate time required: 90 – 180 minutes/day

Notes - Week 9:

Week 10: Practising Performing - Step 3

*Never share your hopes and dreams with negative people
– they will only bring you down. Instead, share your hopes and
dreams with positive people – they will help you up.*

Goals for this week:

- Continue with 30 Minutes of Motion every day
- Continue with Free Writing
- Continue to make use of your Snap Shot
- Continue with Qi Gong or Tai Chi (if time permits)
- Continue to Add Value to your own life and the lives of others
- Continue 5 Sense Visualisation, using your Mantra and Pre-Performance Rituals
- Continue to experiment with silence
- Begin Practising Performing – Step 3
- Experiment with Going Peripheral and/or 'E=mc^2' and/or Feigning confidence
- Use Cue Cards

Practising Performing – Step 3

This week you will continue with the technique of Practising Performing, and step things up a notch by performing to a recording device. Again, refer back to Chapter 24 to double-check the best way to do this. You may also include the techniques of Going Peripheral, 'E=mc^2', Pre-Performance Rituals and using a Mantra when practising. In addition, begin to experiment with the technique of Feigning Confidence when Practising Performing to a recording device.

Feigning Confidence

You can also incorporate Feigning Confidence in everyday situations. One situation where you might experiment with this technique is when out shopping. Using the advice in Chapter 12, approach a shop assistant and ask them to demonstrate a particular product or article of clothing to you. You don't even need to buy it! The experience of Feigning Confidence in everyday situations can build some strong positive habits that you can transfer to your performing life.

A short note here – don't confuse confidence with arrogance. Be respectful and charming! Note the reactions that you receive from other people when you appear confident, compared to when you appear less confident, uncertain, or unsure of yourself.

Some actors, such as Al Pacino and Tom Cruise, standing at only 168cm, and 172cm respectively, can appear as giants on screen and in real life. Why? They are able to portray immense confidence! When Al Pacino or Tom Cruise are acting, there is absolutely no doubt – they are confidence personified! Are they feigning confidence? We don't know! And that's the point!

Your assignments for this week:

1. Exercise – 30 Minutes of Motion every day – enjoy being alive – move and stretch!!
2. Free Writing – 15 minutes, undisturbed
3. Visualisation: Use your Snap Shot at least 3 times per day.
4a. Practise Qi Gong as described in this book or extend the exercise by attending a class or taking private lessons. Alternatively, practise Tai Chi. Practise preferably twice per day, for 15 minutes at a time

and/or

4b. Continue 5 Sense Visualisation, using your Pre-Performance Rituals
5. Add value to your life and the lives of others every single day
6. Continue experimenting with silence
7. Practising Performing – Step 3, using your Mantra and other Pre-Performance Rituals, and including the techniques of Going Peripheral and/or 'E=mc²' and/or 'Feigning Confidence'
8. Use Cue Cards
9. Make notes in your performance journal

Approximate time required: 90 – 180 minutes/day

Notes - Week 10:

_____

_____

_____

_____

_____

_____

_____

_____

_____

Week 11:   Practising Performing - Step 4

Knowledge is everywhere – in every book, in every person, in every situation. All you have to do is be open enough to receive it.

Goals for this week:

- Continue with 30 Minutes of Motion every day
- Continue with Free Writing
- Continue to make use of your Snap Shot
- Continue with Qi Gong or Tai Chi (if time permits)
- Continue to Add Value to your own life and the lives of others
- Continue 5 Sense Visualisation, using your Mantra and Pre-Performance Rituals
- Continue to experiment with silence
- Begin Practising Performing – Step 4
- Use Cue Cards, if appropriate
- Experiment with Going Peripheral and/or 'E=mc^2' and/or 'Feigning Confidence' and/or 'Role Play'

Practising Performing – Step 4

Following 10 weeks of momentum building, you're now in great shape to advance to Practising Performing – Step 4. That is, practising performing to a small group of friends or colleagues. Review Chapter 24. Remember you can request that your chosen audience refrain from commenting after your performance/s. Or, you may request positive feedback in the form of constructive criticism. In this case, politely request that your audience tells you firstly what it is they liked or enjoyed about your performance, or the way that you performed. Secondly, they may suggest ways that you might improve your performance, or simply inform about certain parts of your performance that you may consider giving some extra polish.

You can even request that your audience adopt the Worst Case Scenario – No Holds Barred! technique of performer distraction. This is of course completely up to you.

Rest as needed

You may choose to carry out your performance to your audience once, twice, or even several times during the week. However do note that if your performance is physically demanding, it may be wise to offer simply a small section of your performance, or to execute Practise Performing – Step 4, only once or twice during the course of the week, allowing for plenty of rest.

Role Play

You may also elect to incorporate the technique of Role-Play in your practise. In this technique, as discussed in Chapter 27, you step into the role of a performer that you admire. How would he/she perform in this situation? What would he/she do? How would he/she stand, sit, talk, gesture, breathe, and act? 'Become' your role model!

Performance journal

Remember also to take note of the effects of the techniques that you are experimenting with in your performance journal. Which ones work best for you? Keep going! You are on the right track!

Your assignments for this week:

wk 11

1. Exercise – 30 Minutes of Motion every day – enjoy being alive – move and stretch!!
2. Free Writing – 15 minutes, undisturbed
3. Visualisation: Use your Snap Shot at least 3 times per day.
4a. Practise Qi Gong as described in this book or extend the exercise by attending a class or taking private lessons. Alternatively, practise Tai Chi. Practise preferably twice per day, for 15 minutes at a time

and/or

4b. Continue 5 Sense Visualisation, using your Pre-Performance Rituals and Mantra
5. Add value to your life and the lives of others every single day
6. Continue experimenting with silence
7. Practising Performing – Step 4, using your Mantra and other Pre-Performance Rituals, and including the techniques of Going Peripheral and/or 'E=mc²' and/or 'Feigning Confidence', and/or 'Role Play'
8. Use Cue Cards
9. Make notes in your performance journal

Approximate time required: 90 – 180 minutes/day

Performing in The Zone

Notes - Week 11:

168

Performing in The Zone

Notes - Week 11:

168

www.thezonebook.com

Week 12:   Practising Performing - Step 5

So, what do you do?
I am.

Goals for this week:
- Continue with 30 Minutes of Motion every day
- Continue with Free Writing
- Continue to make use of your Snap Shot
- Continue with Qi Gong or Tai Chi (if time permits)
- Continue to Add Value to your own life and the lives of others
- Continue 5 Sense Visualisation, using your Mantra and Pre-Performance Rituals
- Continue to experiment with silence
- Begin Practising Performing – Step 5
- Use Cue Cards
- Consolidate – choose the techniques you want to use for your coming performance.

Practising Performing – Step 5
In Week 12, it's time to consolidate. Which of the techniques that you have experimented with so far seem to work best for you? In your performance coming up at the end of this week, which techniques could you utilise to help you get closer to performing in The Zone?

Public, private, or a recording?
Remember that your performance at the end of this week doesn't necessarily have to be a public one. You can organise a small, private audience made up of friends, family, or colleagues if you wish, and present your performance to them.

If giving a public or private performance seems too daunting for you at this stage, then presenting your performance to a recording device, as in Practising Performing – Step 3, will certainly make you feel more at ease.

Whether your performance at the end of this week is public, private, or to a recording device, it's important to have the date and time for your performance set – a concrete goal to work towards. In this way you also know that you'll be able to give yourself some well-earned time off when your performance is complete!

It's a process
If you haven't been 100% honest with yourself during The 12 Week Performance Success Programme and perhaps haven't followed through with all of the exercises, tools, techniques, or maybe even missed some days or even weeks during the

programme, it's not the end of the world! Getting to The Zone is a process – one which takes different approaches, as well as different periods of time, for all of us.

Whether you in fact reach The Zone in your performance at the end of Week 12 is not as important as you may think. What really matters is that you make **improvement towards performing in The Zone.** By concentrating on finding solutions to achieving an ideal level of performance arousal, and becoming open to new possibilities and ideas to help you improve your state of mind in performing situations, you can succeed in your goal of optimal performance in The Zone. By diligently following The 12 Week Performance Success Programme from beginning to end and going through with this process, you will at the very least have set wheels in motion.

And finally, remember that by performing, you are adding value to your own life as well as the lives of countless others. Enjoy your performance!

Your assignments for this week:

1. Exercise – 30 Minutes of Motion every day – enjoy being alive – move and stretch!!
2. Free Writing – 15 minutes, undisturbed
3. Visualisation: Use your Snap Shot at least 3 times per day.
4a Practise Qi Gong as described in this book or extend the exercise by attending a class or taking private lessons. Alternatively, practise Tai Chi. Practise preferably twice per day, for 15 minutes at a time

and/or

4b. Continue 5 Sense Visualisation, using your Pre-Performance Rituals
5. Add value to your life and the lives of others every single day
6. Continue experimenting with silence
7. Consolidate: Decide on which techniques you want to use for your coming performance.
8. Practising Performing – Step 5, now including only the Pre-Performance Rituals, Mantra, and other techniques that you have chosen for your coming performance.
9. Use Cue Cards
10. Make notes in your performance journal

Approximate time required: 90 – 180 minutes/day

Notes - Week 12:

171

wk 12

35. The 12 Week Performance Success Programme - Self assessment

The 12 Week Performance Success Programme contains a lot of information, tools, techniques, and exercises which can help you take some considerable steps towards performing in The Zone. When you have completed The 12 Week Performance Success Programme and given your final performance at the end of the 12th week, it is time to execute the third and fourth steps of the 4 Step Success Strategy. For Step 3, self-assessment, look back now at your performance journal, examine your notes, and then answer the following questions.

35. Exercise: Self assessment

Which techniques/exercises were the most effective for me?

_____

_____

_____

Which of these techniques/exercises can I use in my next performance?

_____

_____

_____

3

Which techniques/exercises were the least effective for me, and could be taken away from this programme when I go through it the next time?

_____

_____

_____

Which techniques could I add (or experiment with further) to make this programme even more effective for me?

_____

_____

_____

How did I develop during the past 12 weeks? What did I learn?

_____

_____

_____

35. What now?

If you have studied and followed through with The 12 Week Performance Success Programme, practised the tools and techniques with diligence, and undertaken all of the exercises and assignments given, your performance arousal level should be more appropriate in your performance situations, allowing you to perform in or at least closer to The Zone. If you took just one step closer to The Zone as a result of these past 12 weeks – congratulations! You are on the right path!

Options - Step 4

After now having completed The 12 Week Performance Success Programme and self assessment, there are many options open to you. The first of which is to take Step 4 of the 4 Step Success Strategy and re-examine The 12 Week Performance Success Programme from the beginning. Make some changes to the programme based on your self assessment. How can you improve on the programme? Would it work better for you if it was longer? Shorter? Or incorporated different techniques and exercises? Design your own Performance Success Programme for your own specific performing needs. Begin your programme, follow it through to the end, assess it, make further adjustments if necessary, and follow through your programme again. This constant refining process can be a powerful way to further help your development towards an ideal state of mind for your performing situations.

Options - Being coached

Another very effective way to continue your journey to The Zone is to enlist the help of your own private coach. You can seek out the help of a coach in your area, or request private coaching through www.thezonebook.com

Options - Coaching others

You may decide that the process of learning to control your own performance arousal level and reaching for The Zone is so rewarding that you want to help others. If you're in this situation, one way to help encourage or motivate your friends and colleagues is to inform them of the website www.thezonebook.com where they can pick up their own copy of *Performing in The Zone*. You may then like to encourage them to experiment with the techniques in Part Two of *Performing in The Zone*, and help them follow through with their own 12 Week Performance Success Programme. This is a fantastic way of adding value to your own life as well as the lives of others

PART FOUR
Digging Deeper

37
38
39
40
41
42
43
44
45

37. The Emotional Handbrake

Completing the exercises, using the tools and techniques, and following through with
The 12 Week Performance Success Programme contained within this book may be all
you ever need to achieve an ideal level of performance arousal, enabling you to
consistently perform in The Zone. However if you still find yourself several steps
away from performing in The Zone after having completed the 12 Week Performance
Success Programme at least once or twice, and diligently applying the exercises and
techniques provided, don't fret!

Internal barriers - The emotional handbrake

Occasionally we experience blocks, only to have everything 'click' when we least
expect it. It is not unusual to experience these internal blocks or mental barriers in
your journey to The Zone. Be patient – you can and will succeed!

Firstly, remember that if you've come this far and discovered that you have taken one
or more steps towards more controlled performance arousal, you are on the right
track! Reward yourself!

Secondly, the process of controlling performance arousal and performing in The Zone
can sometimes take longer than originally expected. Give yourself the time you need
to take further steps in the right direction.

And thirdly, this part of *Performing in The Zone* has been specially included to provide
you with some additional sources of help and advice in your journey to optimal
performance. By examining these complimentary sources outlined here, you may
very well find the answers you are looking for.

A charmed past

There are very few of us who have what one would consider a 'charmed' past. By
charmed I mean a life thus far filled only with 100% positive experiences – a life growing
up in the perfect encouraging family, learning from the best teachers, experiencing an
ideal school environment, associating with the most fantastic and supportive peer
group, living in the safest neighbourhood, and so on.

Defence mechanism

According to the philosophy of the Rosen Therapy holistic treatment method (among
others), we as humans possess a 'defence mechanism' which has the ability to protect
ourselves at times when we undergo the various negative experiences, emotional
stresses, and traumas in our lives.

This 'defence mechanism' can be manifested physically as tension in various parts of the
body, helping us cope with both mildly negative as well as more traumatic experiences

when they occur. However, the 'defence mechanisms' created to help us in times of strife can in fact cause us problems later on if we are unable to 'switch them off' or release them when they are not needed. If this happens, the emotional stresses and physical tensions built up during negative times can become ingrained in our behaviour, affecting many parts of our lives, including our state of mind before and during performing situations.

Baggage

In other words, if you haven't been able to fully deal with the negative experiences of your past, it is possible that you can be carrying around some sort of emotional baggage, blockages, or internal barriers, whether you are aware of this or not. These barriers may be preventing you from achieving an ideal state of mind in your performing situations.

Driving with the handbrake on

One way of thinking about the concept of holding on to old emotional baggage and internal barriers is driving a car with the handbrake on. You can still get to certain places, but it might be a struggle. Moreover you avoid the biggest hills because you 'know' that the climb will be too tough – something along the way may overheat, get worn out, or even break down completely.

Solutions

So how do you release the emotional handbrake – old physical and psychological tensions – to allow yourself the best possible chance of fully achieving your true potential, climbing the hill as it were, obtaining an ideal state of mind for your performing situations, and performing in The Zone? There are no simple answers to this question, as we are all different, have all experienced various events in the past – both positive and negative, and have handled these events in a variety of ways. The exercises, tools, and techniques in Part Two of this book, and The 12 Week Performance Success Programme in Part 3 may have provided you with a partial solution. However, there are also many other complimentary sources of advice and help that you can explore. A selection of these alternative sources of help can be found here in this part of *Performing in The Zone*.

38. Diet and Exercise

Disclaimer: The information given below is in no way intended to replace specialist medical advice provided by a health professional. Should you suspect that you have a health problem you should visit a health professional immediately.

Your body and your brain are beautifully constructed. They are arguably the most complex and sophisticated pieces of 'machinery' in our known universe. Unfortunately however, neither came with an instruction manual! Understanding how our minds and bodies work, and indeed interact, has been the subject of countless studies. In fact the amount of written material available about diet and exercise alone is simply mind-blowing, and therefore discussing the complete conclusions of this material would be far beyond the scope of this book. However, here follows some practical advice about the effects of diet and exercise on performance arousal.

Your diet and performance arousal

As you now know, performing in The Zone is a state of mind. Your state of mind, and therefore your performance arousal level, can be considerably affected by the foods and drinks that you consume.

How does this work?

When digested, the nutrients from the foods and drinks that you consume enter your bloodstream. Along with the air you breathe, these nutrients provide nourishment for your body and brain.

The three worst offenders

With regards to performance arousal, it has been found that certain substances can have strong negative effects on your state of mind in performing situations, especially when consumed in large doses. The three worst offenders here are:
- alcohol
- refined sugar
- caffeine

These three substances directly affect the chemicals in your body and your brain, and can in turn affect your mood, as well as the way you think, feel, perceive, experience, and react in performing and non-performing situations alike. Consuming an excess of alcohol, refined sugar, and caffeine can cause an artificial activation of your Sympathetic Nervous System. This can quite simply lead to increased levels of both chronic and acute anxiety, nervousness, and over-excitement. These are all states of mind which can prevent you from achieving an optimal level of performance! In addition, to those who have become highly dependent upon alcohol, refined sugar, or caffeine, depression can ensue if these substances are suddenly unavailable.

Examine your diet

Think about your own diet. What do you consume over the course of an average week? Do you regularly consume any of the above substances, and in addition have trouble maintaining an optimum level of performance arousal for your performing situations? If so, gradually begin to cut down on foods and drinks containing these substances, with the intention of eventually abstaining from them altogether. If you have the will-power, remove these substances from your diet completely. Again, Chapter 5 can be helpful here.

Food allergies – the wrong 'fuels' for your 'engine'

Some of us are allergic to certain foods. If we consume the foods that our bodies do not tolerate, classic allergies such as nut allergies can clearly, and at times violently, make their presence felt. If your body has a strong reaction to a food such as nuts, you probably don't need to be told to avoid this type of food!

However, some of us can experience milder or delayed reactions to certain foods. Lactose and gluten intolerance for example can take on both aggressive and at times more subtle forms. We can also have abnormal reactions to artificial chemicals in foods, such as artificial flavourings, colourings, sweeteners, preservatives, and certain 'E-numbers'. These reactions and sensitivities can have an affect our mood.

Seemingly minor digestive problems as a result of food allergies or intolerances can cause serious negative effects for your body and mind if experienced over a longer period of time. These negative effects can have a direct impact on your state of mind in daily life, as well as your performance arousal level in performing situations.

If you are uncertain whether or not you are affected by food allergies, it is best to make an appointment with a health professional or testing laboratory to find out exactly which foods you should avoid, if any.

Nutrients and Mivitotal Plus

We all require a myriad of various vitamins, minerals, and essential fatty acids to maintain healthy functioning of the body and mind. In an ideal world, all of the nutrients we require would come from the foods we eat. However, due to various reasons such as modern herbicides and pesticides, soils and feed with low nutrient content, poor diets, over-cooked foods, artificial additives, improperly combined foods, or simply avoiding meals, you may be lacking some of the key nutritional elements you require for optimum mental and physical health. This may be making your journey to The Zone unnecessarily difficult. Unfortunately in our modern, intensive, and 'factory-farming' society, almost all of us require alternative sources of nutrition for healthy functioning. Perhaps the simplest way to ensure that you are receiving the nutrients you require is by taking a high-quality nutritional supplement. There are so many vitamin and mineral supplements available to us in the international marketplace that it can be a bit mind-boggling knowing exactly which to choose. Also, as with the majority of health products, quality and price of vitamin and mineral supplements can vary enormously.

As a starting point for your nutritional well-being, I'd like to recommend here Mivitotal Plus – a high-concentrate vitamin and mineral supplement available from Hela Pharma AB in Sweden. For more information about Mivitotal Plus, and to find out how you can order it, send an email to info@mivitotal.se (in English or Swedish) or visit their website at www.mivitotal.se (currently in Swedish only). For other effective vitamin and mineral supplements, consult with your doctor, pharmacist, nutritionist, or other qualified health professional.

Dietary changes

It has been proven by several studies that significant improvement in a wide range of physical and mental health problems can result from examining ones diet, and making changes where necessary. In the realms of mental health alone, when diet has been analysed and modified, improvements have been recorded in people suffering from the following conditions: mood swings, anxiety, panic attacks, depression, irritability, aggression, concentration, memory problems, premenstrual syndrome (PMS), obsessive-compulsive feelings, insomnia, fatigue, behavioural and learning disorders, and seasonal affective disorder (SAD). As performing in The Zone is a state of mind, it stands to reason therefore that making changes in your diet where necessary can have significant benefits for you in controlling the levels of performance arousal you experience.

Your current diet may be a contributing factor preventing you from achieving an ideal state of mind in your performing situations. To receive specialised dietary information for you, your body type, and your performing situations, it can be of great benefit to visit a dietician or nutritionist experienced in advising successful sports people. As an alternative, you may like to visit a healthcare professional experienced in prescribing dietary changes for treating people with anxiety and other related mental health issues.

Exercise, stress, and performance arousal

If you are prone to performance anxiety, engaging in regular physical activity – exercise – can have a profound improvement on your performance arousal level.

When you feel stressed in day to day situations, adrenaline is pumped into your bloodstream, and can cause you to experience anxiety, or as we've already seen, the 'Fight or Flight' response. If you feel the effects of stress for large parts of your day, over a period of weeks, months, or even years, this prolonged underlying 'Fight or Flight' can have severe negative consequences on your performance arousal level in performing situations.

Although stress usually goes hand-in-hand with the modern Western urban lifestyle, it does not necessarily need to be the case. You can indeed lower your stress levels and thereby alleviate anxiety by engaging in **regular physical activity.** By exercising, you provide a natural way for your body and mind to release tension.

By simply engaging in gentle exercise as soon as you wake up, you can set yourself up mentally and physically for the rest of the day, alleviate stress, melt anxiety, and even help to prevent it from reoccurring in performing situations. This is the primary reason that 30 Minutes of Motion has been included in The 12 Week Performance Success Programme, and put at the top of the list for every single week.

Different types of exercise

Any type of physical movement that increases your heart rate, oxygen intake and blood circulation can be labelled as exercise. When discussing exercise, we can talk about three main categories:

1. Stretches and flexibility exercises, for improving the range of motion and ease of movement for your muscles and joints
2. Aerobic exercise, for toning muscles and increasing cardiovascular endurance. Aerobic exercise involves low intensity activities performed for longer periods of time, such as cycling, walking, jogging, swimming, and circuit training.
3. Anaerobic exercise, for building muscle strength and mass. Anaerobic exercise involves intense muscular effort carried out over short periods of time, such as power lifting, other forms of weight training, and sprinting.

All forms of exercise can have positive benefits for both the body and mind.

More about the benefits of exercise on the mind

The physical benefits of exercise have long been known, and are well documented. These benefits include better muscle tone, increased joint flexibility, stronger bones, an increased resistance to injury, prevention of disease, regulation of blood pressure, a stronger immune system, and a more efficient metabolism. In addition, it has been well documented that exercise can have strong benefits for the mind.

When we exercise, engage in deep breathing, meditation, or laugh, our bodies produce chemicals called endorphins, as well as a recently discovered chemical called phenylethylamine. These chemicals appear to produce noticeable benefits on the mind, including:

- Reduction in stress
- Reduction in anxiety
- Reduced depression
- Improved capacity for cognition
- Improved mood
- Relaxation

Also, by exercising we improve our physical appearance by burning excess fat, improving our skin and muscle tone, and can even avoid premature ageing. These physical effects can help improve our confidence, thereby steering us away from negative thought processes which may have been a root cause of negative performance arousal (anxiety) in our performing situations. It has even been discovered that exercise can have the equivalent benefits of pharmaceutical drugs for depression as well as treatments in psychotherapy. This is why exercise is now being prescribed as a treatment for certain mental illnesses in the U.K.

As you can see, the psychological benefits of exercise are wide ranging.

Exercise and sleep

Sleep apnea and sleep deprivation can lead to negative effects on our overall level of physical and mental performance. It can also lead to us experiencing strong feelings of negative performance arousal. Therefore, to perform at your best, it is important that you take measures to ensure that you sleep soundly. This is where the final and very important benefit of exercise comes in.

We tend to sleep more soundly and wake up more refreshed when we exercise regularly. This is due to the increase in the flow of blood and oxygen to the brain that we can experience as a result of regular exercise, as well as the relaxation response triggered after a workout.

If you suspect you are suffering from sleep apnea or sleep deprivation, initiating a gentle and regular exercise programme may help you to sleep more soundly, allowing your body a better chance to rest, and your giving your mind a better chance to focus and concentrate in performing situations, allowing you easier access to performing in The Zone.

Putting it together: Your Body Mass Index (BMI)

By eating an appropriate diet and exercising regularly, you can set up a strong foundation for getting in the right state of mind for any performing situation, giving you a stronger likelihood of performing in The Zone. Along with bringing your performance arousal level under control, an appropriate diet and regular exercise can also help you obtain an improved weight/height balance – a balance which can be represented by a number on a scale known as BMI – Body Mass Index.

38

BMI is an approximate measure, and does not take into account body fat or muscle mass. However the Body Mass Index does serve to provide a basic image of your ideal weight/height ratio, and can even provide clues about performance arousal.

The formula to work out your BMI using metric measurements is:

$$BMI = \frac{\text{weight (kg)}}{\text{height}^2 \text{ (m}^2)}$$

The formula to use for imperial measurements (U.K. and U.S.) is:

$$BMI = \frac{\text{weight (lbs) x 703}}{\text{height}^2 \text{ (in}^2)}$$

Using your own weight and height in the above formulae, you can come up with a number which is your BMI. The following chart shows how your resulting BMI number relates to your weight category:

Category	BMI Range (kg/m^2 or lbs/in^2)
Severely Underweight	Less than 16.5
Underweight	16.5 – 18.5
Normal	**18.5 – 25**
Overweight	25 – 30
Obese	30 or more

So for example, a person with a height of 175cm (69 in) weighing in at 72kg (159 lbs) would have a BMI of 23.5 – a weight considered normal for their height.

What about you?

Where do you fall in the BMI weight category range? If you have problems maintaining an ideal level of performance arousal in your performing situations, and find that you are underweight or overweight according to the above chart, adjusting your diet and the amount of exercise you carry out each day may help. By changing your diet if necessary and exercising regularly, you can both reach your ideal weight, and allow yourself easier access to performing in The Zone.

A disturbing fact

The results of a recent national health and nutrition survey in the U.S. discovered that 63% of Americans have a BMI of 25 or more (overweight), with 26% falling into the obese category.

An inspirational figure

Jack LaLanne, 'The Godfather of Fitness', was born in 1914, and at the time of the writing of this book, still exercises for a full 2 hours every day, at 94 years of age. Jack is living proof of his own quote: "Exercise is King, nutrition is Queen. Put them together and you've got a kingdom."

A sugar addict at 15, Jack made the decision to completely change his diet and begin to exercise after attending a lecture by revolutionary nutritionist, Paul Bragg. Jack stopped consuming sugar and white flour altogether, and concentrated on building a strong and flexible body – a drive stemmed from an immensely positive mind. Jack's many and amazing achievements to date are documented at his website www.jacklalanne.com However for inspirational purposes I'd like to highlight a few here:

- Jack opened the USA's first modern health studio in 1936
- He presented a daily TV show about diet and exercise for over 30 years

- On his 70th birthday, Jack swam towing 70 boats with 70 people from the Queen's Way Bridge in the Long Beach Harbour to the Queen Mary, a distance of 1 ½ miles, whilst handcuffed and shackled and in strong winds and currents.
- Jack has a star on the Hollywood hall of fame
- **At the age of 94, Jack still works out for a full 2 hours every day!**

The good news is that you don't need to be towing boats in stormy seas every day to reach The Zone in your field of performance! However, maintaining a healthy body and mind are prerequisites for any performer in their journey to The Zone. According to Jack LaLanne, you too, despite your current age or physical condition, can improve your physical and mental health through correct diet and regular exercise. And by doing this, you can ensure the best possible pre-requisites for bringing your performance arousal level under control, allowing you to unlock your full potential and perform in The Zone.

Diet and exercise: Summing it all up

Exercising regularly and maintaining the correct diet for your body can help you to achieve an optimum level of performance arousal for your performing situations. Here are the main points from this chapter – some basic dietary and exercise advice – which may help you get closer to performing in The Zone:

Basic dietary advice:

- Avoid all caffeinated and artificially sweetened foods and beverages, especially on performance days, as these can cause an artificial and at times uncontrollable activation of your Sympathetic Nervous System, resulting in performance anxiety.
- Take a food allergy test. Find out which foods you should avoid completely.
- Use daily vitamin and mineral supplements such as Mivitotal Plus.
- Eat little or no fast 'food'.
- Make sure a large part of your diet consists of fresh, raw, or lightly cooked natural foods.
- Ensure that foods with a high fluid content comprise a significant part of your diet.
- Maintain a balance of acidic and alkaline foods.
- Combine foods correctly whenever possible using the laws of trophology as discussed in Daniel Reid's *The Tao of Health, Sex and Longevity* – Chapter 1, Diet and Nutrition.
- Never overeat – stop when you feel 80% full.

Basic exercise/motion advice:

- Exercise regularly – whether it be a simple 30 Minutes of Motion every day, some basic stretches, or a more intense workout.
- Choose a physical activity that you enjoy!
- Choose a physical activity that you have easy access to.
- Try individual activities such as swimming and cycling, as well as group based exercise such as basketball, volleyball, or other team sports.
- Begin learning a soft-style martial art such as Ki Aikido – in this way you can train your mind, body, and learn self-defence!
- Carry out the full range of motion in all of your muscles and joints every day.
- Invent your own exercise programme or get specialist advice from a personal trainer.
- Exercise with a partner to help with motivation.
- Throw away your T.V. – **exercise instead of becoming just another couch potato!**

Some highly recommended sources of further information about diet and exercise

Jack LaLanne:
All audio, video, and written publications
www.jacklalanne.com

Daniel Reid:
The Tao of Health, Sex and Longevity
ISBN: 0-7434-0907-8

Paul and Patricia Bragg:
Bragg Healthy Lifestyle
ISBN: 0-8779-0004-3

Using this basic diet and exercise advice, and by studying the teachings of diet and exercise masters such as Jack LaLanne, Daniel Reid, and Paul and Patricia Bragg, you can create some solid foundations to allow yourself easier access to The Zone. And what's more, you can prolong and improve the quality of your whole life! Quality diet and regular exercise are the best health insurance policies available, and an important part of helping you to perform in The Zone!

38

39. Traditional Chinese Medicine (TCM)

Background

Traditional Chinese Medicine (TCM) is the Western name given to the multifaceted traditional treatment method which originated in China more than 3000 years ago. TCM theories are based on: balance – *Yin* and *Yang*, meridians – *Jing Lou,* energy – *Qi,* and internal organs, *Zang.* Using TCM theory, a less than ideal level of performance arousal in a performing situation constitutes a state of imbalance – something that can be rectified with correct diagnosis and treatment.

Therefore, although primarily a medicinal practise, TCM can offer considerable assistance in achieving peak physical performance, as well as an ideal mental state for performing situations.

Diagnosis and Treatment

Several different forms of diagnosis exist within TCM, including pulse diagnosis, tongue diagnosis, questions about the effects of the patient's problem, observations of any bodily odours, as well as other unobtrusive clinical observations.

The most common forms of treatment in TCM include: Acupuncture, Tui Na massage, moxibustion, cupping, herbal medicine, and the holistic exercise form known as medicinal Qi Gong. All forms of TCM work by returning the body's systems to their natural and correct state of balance, thereby curing both acute and chronic conditions. A master TCM practitioner can use various techniques to exert control over and divert energy or 'Qi' towards, or away from various parts of the body, depending upon the ailment and treatment required.

Practitioners

In China as well as an increasing number of Western countries, the study of TCM is taken very seriously, with most TCM doctors completing several years of intense education followed by further supervised clinical experience, before entering the profession as fully fledged TCM practitioners. However in some countries it is possible to attend a weekend seminar in order to obtain 'certification' in fields such as acupuncture. Practitioners with such a limited education, even with the best of intentions, are unfortunately grossly unqualified, and should be avoided. Therefore, when looking for a TCM practitioner, be sure to ask about their qualifications and experience.

Acupuncture

Acupuncture is one of the most powerful and accessible branches of Traditional Chinese Medicine, and can be of considerable help for performers. It is a common misconception that acupuncture is purely used for pain relief and to treat physical symptoms. Acupuncture is in fact equally effective as a cure for both physical and psychological problems, as in many cases it simultaneously treats the cause of a problem as well as the manifested symptom or symptoms. The most common ailments treated with acupuncture include:

- Back, neck, and joint problems, including rheumatism
- Pain relief
- Digestion problems, including diarrhoea and constipation
- Allergies, asthma, eczema, sinus inflammation
- Infertility and menstruation problems
- Sports injuries, RSI/OOS, tendon and muscle problems
- Nerve pain, pinched nerves and other associated disorders
- Migraine and stress headaches
- Eating disorders
- Smoking and alcohol dependence
- Depression, sleep disorders, chronic fatigue
- Anxiety

Due to its holistic nature and effectiveness in rebalancing the human energy system, acupuncture can be a powerful complementary source of assistance in your journey to performing in The Zone.

Qi Gong

The word Qi in Chinese (pronounced *tchi*) roughly translates to 'energy', 'breath' or 'air'. Gong (pronounced *gung*) refers to 'work'. Therefore Qi Gong can be approximately translated to 'energy work'.

Chinese scholars have known for several thousand years that the human body is made up of complex energy systems. This knowledge has over the course of the past century filtered through the language and cultural barriers, and is becoming more and more widely accepted here in the West.

Serious distortions in the human energy system can bring about diverse physical and psychological ailments which can include headaches, depression, chronic fatigue syndrome, joint inflammation, and even digestive disorders to name but a few. These ailments can have a profound impact on our level of performance arousal. Qi Gong can be studied and practised for cultivating and balancing energy within the human system. As "energy is everything", by practising Qi Gong and hence exerting control over your own energy system, you can maintain and improve your physical and psychological well-being.

Health Benefits

The health benefits of Qi Gong are widely documented, with the most common being stress reduction and preventative health care through gentle physical motion and controlled breathing. Medicinal Qi Gong is officially recognised as a standard medical technique in Chinese hospitals. Qi Gong can be especially effective in manifesting performance arousal positively at a low and calm level, and is thus most suitable for performers requiring precise control of delicate motor skills in performing situations.

Teachers

Learning Qi Gong from books and videos can be helpful to give a basic understanding of the art form, but as with all martial arts, there is no substitute for a qualified, experienced, and compassionate teacher. Experienced Chinese and non-Chinese Qi Gong teachers can now be found in the majority of cities in the East and West. The absolute best means of finding out exactly what Qi Gong can do for you is to enrol in a class, or enlist the help of a private Qi Gong teacher. Qi Gong is simple to learn and can be carried out by anyone regardless of age, gender, or physical condition. The benefits of Qi Gong are available to all who practise this ancient art form.

If you are a performer requiring low levels of positive performance arousal, or simply wish to gain an overall reduction in stress and anxiety, investigate Qi Gong teachers and classes in your area today!

40. Alexander Technique

Background

During the early period of his career as an actor in the latter part of the 19th century, F. Matthias Alexander developed a severe vocal problem. His hoarseness and loss of voice when performing were affecting him to such an extent that his career was in serious danger of coming to a premature conclusion. Unable to be helped by doctors and specialists at the time, Alexander decided to examine the physical and psychological processes within himself in an attempt to unravel his mysterious, seemingly incurable ailment.

Tension

After a considerable time experimenting with a complex system of mirrors, arranged so that he could observe himself from all angles, Alexander eventually realised that his subconscious mind was creating a sequence of anticipatory tensions throughout his body. This tension process built up as he began to think of the lines he was about to recite. Without the system of mirrors utilised for self-observation, Alexander would not have been aware of this physical tension process, as he was unable to actually feel the process happening.

Allowing it to roll freely

Instead of concentrating his efforts on how he might deliver his lines more effectively by better articulating his words, or projecting more vocal power, Alexander decided to focus on removing the excess tension that he was observing using his mirror system. His aim was to maintain the most efficient use of his body and mind, allowing them to function freely and unhindered. In other words, we might say that instead of driving a car downhill with the handbrake on and gas pedal pressed to the floor, Alexander aimed to release both the handbrake and gas pedal, allowing the car to freely roll down the hill at its natural pace.

Knock-on effects

By directing his body and mind more efficiently, Alexander cured his vocal problems, and developed a more relaxed and resonant voice. He also found that the physical and psychological techniques he developed to cure his vocal problems had an effect on other physical motions in his day to day life. Doctors and specialists soon began to refer other patients with baffling, seemingly incurable physical symptoms to Alexander, who, with gentle correcting motions using his own body, was able to help.

The body/mind connection

Alexander stated that it is impossible to imagine any activity which is purely mental or purely physical. In other words, Alexander was implying that the mind and body are inseparable, and that all actions include both a mental and physical component. Therefore, instead of talking solely about using the body or the mind to complete a task, in Alexander Technique, the holistic term 'self' is preferred. Using this philosophy, Alexander realised that tension in the body is affected by tension in the mind, and vice versa.

The Alexander Technique and performance arousal

In short, when learning the Alexander Technique, you cultivate an awareness of how your mind and body interact in daily activities, as well as your sphere of performance. By learning to direct your body appropriately for a given task, the Alexander Technique makes you aware of appropriate and inappropriate (excess) physical and mental tension, previously unnoticed due to habitual use. By reducing your unnecessary tension, natural, healthy functioning can be restored to your body and mind.

In regards to performance arousal, one might say that according to the Alexander Technique, an inappropriate level of performance arousal can be described as a misuse of the 'self' – i.e. inappropriate muscular and psychological activation for a given activity.

Postural alignment

Your head, neck, and back, make up your postural core according to Alexander Technique. All parts of your physical and mental functioning, including achieving an ideal performance arousal level in your performing situations, can be optimised by improving the natural direction of your body.

In addition, as the Alexander Technique can reduce physical obstructions by allowing for proper alignment of head, neck, spine, larynx and vocal tract, the quality of your breathing can improve. When this happens, symptoms such as anxiety can be reduced, allowing you freer access to The Zone.

Alexander Technique and the 'here and now'

In everyday life as well as performing situations, we can at times have a tendency to keep our mind and actions focussed on an end result whilst losing sight of the means whereby the result is achieved. Using Alexander Technique terminology, this is referred to as 'end-gaining', and is a habit which can build habitual tension and anxiety. By allowing you to focus on the here and now – the process – rather than the outcome of the process, the Alexander Technique can help to avoid 'end-gaining'. By directing your actions, rather than concentrating hard on the outcome of those actions, it is possible to relieve excess physical and mental tension. This is true for both performing and non-performing situations alike.

Anxiety, excitement, and your body

Anxiety and excitement are psycho-physical. That is to say that when excited or anxious, your body is used in a particular way. Alexander Technique can make you become aware of how you direct your body, so that you can obtain the ideal state of 'self' for your performing situations.

Quite simply, Alexander Technique can help you to perform in The Zone by allowing your body and mind to act unhindered.

Teachers

Teachers of the Alexander Technique are generally easy to find in the U.K., continental Europe, North America, and Australia. Before enlisting the help of an Alexander Technique teacher, ensure that they have undergone the minimum of 1600 hours tuition required to become properly qualified and accredited.

In the U.K. the Society of Teachers of the Alexander Technique (STAT) is an ideal place to start your search for a teacher. The STAT website is www.stat.org.uk This website also provides useful information when searching for Alexander Technique teachers in other countries.

40

If you suspect you have physical and/or psychological barriers or tensions preventing you from entering The Zone and performing to your full potential, it may prove worthwhile to seek the help of an experienced Alexander Technique teacher near you.

41. Neuro-Linguistic Programming (NLP)

Background

Neuro-Linguistic Programming or NLP for short, originated in the 1970's as a new method of psychotherapy. The founders John Grinder and Richard Bandler were of the opinion that traditional psychology was all too focussed on 'dysfunctional' personality types, mapping problems, and formulating theories about the origins of these problems. Contrary to other forms of psychology, NLP does not categorise personalities as functional or dysfunctional. Rather, according to NLP, we all have a certain neurology, life experience, and ability to alter our perspective of the world and ourselves. What NLP aims to do is simply guide the brain to the right path for a certain goal – control of performance arousal for example.

NLP is designed to work with your cognitive and emotional processes on a practical and easily understandable level. It concentrates on how your nervous system (neuro) has a specific and complex language (linguistic) in the form of inner pictures, sounds, feelings, and words that it constantly uses to process and understand (programming) reality with.

NLP has many uses, and can be adapted to such diverse fields as psychotherapy, interpersonal communication, sports, and the performance arts.

Perception

Neuro-Linguistic Programming is something that we all use, in every day of our lives. We see inner pictures, hear inner sounds, and have an inner dialog that comments constantly on our experiences. The quality of these inner pictures, sounds, and inner dialog governs whether we feel secure or insecure, confident or unsure, empowered or disempowered, in The Zone or not. According to NLP theory, you create your own understanding of reality, and it is this perceived reality, rather than reality itself, that has a profound effect on how you view and interact with the world around you. Due to this, NLP has become popular in recent years as a way of helping all manner of people overcome their own self-perceived or self-induced problems, whilst respecting their own capabilities.

Changing perception

With the help of specialised NLP techniques, you can change the images, sounds, and inner dialog that constantly runs in your mind. Your perception of reality can be modified, therefore giving you a completely different life experience. The consequences of this shift of perception are quickly reflected in your emotional state, and can give fast and measurable results in every aspect of your life.

There are a large number of powerful techniques available to NLP practitioners. Below are two fundamental techniques.

Chapter 41

NLP Technique – Empowering Questions

As mentioned previously, your mind is like a powerful super-computer. If you ask it questions, it will do everything it can to come up with answers. Therefore, the quality of the questions you ask it has immense bearing on your perception of reality. You are capable of asking yourself and others both empowering and disempowering questions.

Examples of disempowering questions are:
"What's wrong?"
"Why is this a problem?"
"Why did this happen?"
"Why don't you understand?"
"Why does this always happen to me?"

Using the technique of empowering questions, these questions can be rephrased in the following way:
"What would I like instead of my current situation?"
"How can I solve this?"
"What can I do to prevent this situation from occurring again?"
"How can I express myself so that you can understand me more easily?"
"What can I learn from this to ensure that this never happens again?"

By asking yourself and others empowering questions, you open a door to receive positive, empowering answers.

41

NLP Technique – Anchoring

Have you even heard a song on the radio that instantly 'takes you back' to a certain time or place in your mind? Perhaps a 'Summer' song, which brings back the relaxed feeling of that special holiday in the sun all those years ago? Or perhaps you've been walking in a crowd, and noticed the doft of a specific perfume that instantly reminds you of a certain person, bringing back fond and warm memories? These are examples of what is known in NLP as positive anchors. Using the NLP technique of anchoring, you can create your own positive anchors to be called upon when in a performing situation.

Creating and using anchors

To create a positive anchor, you stimulate one of your senses in a unique way when feeling at an ideal state of performance arousal. For example, in a practise session, you firstly get yourself into an ideal state of performance arousal, using some of the techniques outlined in Part Two if necessary. You then carry out a unique action such as smelling the doft from a certain bottle of perfume, saying a particular word or phrase, or carrying out a specific physical motion. The idea here is that when you reach this ideal level of performance arousal, and carry out this unique action enough times in practise sessions, it will create the positive anchor.

Then, prior to a real performance situation, you simply carry out this action again – either smell the perfume, say the word or phrase, or carry out the physical motion – to bring you instantly back to the level of performance arousal you experienced in the practise environment. The anchor 'takes you back' to the ideal level of performance arousal you had practised earlier, and you achieve a performance in The Zone.

You may like to find out more about Neuro-Linguistic Programming and how it can help you to reach The Zone by searching for certified NLP practitioners in your local area. Alternatively, you may like to start by using an audio programme, as outlined in the next chapter.

42. Audio Programmes

As mentioned in The 12 Week Performance Success Programme, "Knowledge is everywhere – in every book, in every person, in every situation. All you have to do is be open enough to receive it." One way to receive knowledge to help you in your journey to performing in The Zone is from audio programmes. Many audio programmes have been made available since the explosion of digital media. Some of these sources of information are fantastic, whilst others are perhaps not all you would expect. However, if you are open to different forms of knowledge from the various sources available, you will quickly find out which sources work best for you.

A starting point

You may like to begin with the audio programme *Practising Performing*. This programme is specifically designed to help you as a performer achieve optimal results in your field of performance, and can be downloaded at www.thezonebook.com

43. Get a Personal Coach

By going it alone, the techniques and exercises in this book can help you to take control of your performance arousal level, bringing about some fantastic results by getting you closer to The Zone in your field of performance. In addition, having a personal coach to encourage, support, and motivate you along your path to The Zone can provide a powerful additional source of help.

Different roles

Many successful sports teams and individual sports people employ the service of dedicated, knowledgeable, and experienced coaches. A coach may fill several roles – expert, trainer, motivator, mentor or even therapist. Different coaches employ different strategies but the end goal is always the same – to help bring out the best in their athletes, or rather, to help the athletes bring out the best in themselves.

Different guises

Coaches can also come in many other guises. For example, your partner, children, friends, family, or colleagues may be your best sources of motivation, encouragement, and support – the best coaches – for you in your current situation. In addition, specialist lifestyle coaches, motivational speakers, and therapists with experience in specific mental training strategies such as Neuro-Linguistic Programming (NLP), can be of immense benefit.

Being coached

If you already have a coach, show them a copy of this book. Alternatively, you could direct your coach to www.thezonebook.com where they can pick up their own copy. Ask your coach to read through *Performing in The Zone*, and get them to see if there are parts of this book that they could help you with.

If you don't already have a coach, regardless of your ability and experience, and regardless of how your level of performance arousal is manifested, you could benefit from having a private coach or mentor.

You can seek out the help of a professional coach in your area, enlist the alternative approach of having friends, family or colleagues to provide support, inspiration, and motivation for you, or request private coaching through www.thezonebook.com

44. Become a Personal Coach

Perhaps by reading this book so far you may have been inspired to help others, and pursue personal coaching yourself? By becoming a coach for another performer, you invariably 'practise what you preach'. Teaching and coaching others is one of the best ways to learn more about yourself and improve your own knowledge in any field of performance. Some may even state that we learn more from teaching others than we do from being taught.

There's always something to offer

Regardless of the level you feel you have currently achieved in your field of performance, there is always something that you have which can be offered to someone else. The responsibility of coaching others can lead you to making significant discoveries in all aspects of your field of performance, and indeed life in general.

Benefits for all

The very gesture of providing support or motivation for a fellow performer may be all that is required to help that colleague control their performance arousal level and enter The Zone. By being part of this process, you may learn something about yourself as well. Of course the motivation to become a coach shouldn't be purely self fulfilment – rather, this is merely a positive side-effect! By coaching, whether it be direct in the form of actual teaching or instruction, or indirect in the form of offering moral support, you are adding value to someone else's life, as well as your own.

Performing in The Zone

45. A Final Thought...

The following extract from an ancient Greek legend was as true in the antiquity as it is today, and is particularly relevant in regards to achieving an ideal level of performance arousal for your performing situations:

God 1:
"Let us put the answers to life on top of a mountain.
They will never look for them there."

200

Other gods:
"No! They will find them right away."

God 2:
"Let us put the answers to life in the centre of the Earth.
They will never look for them there."

Other gods:
"No! They will find them right away."

God 3:
"Let us put the answers to life at the bottom of the sea.
They will never look for them there."

Other gods:
"No! They will find them right away."

God 4:
"Let us put the answers to life within them.
They will never look for them there!"

And so they did.

www.thezonebook.com

Conclusion

$$RLP = (c + p - e) + a$$

The above equation, originally derived in *Mind and Body: A Theory for Understanding Levels of Musical Performance* in 2002, explains why we all perform at different levels. It shows that the level at which we perform is a result of 4 main factors: what we know about the specifics of our performance sphere 'c', our physical ability to carry out our thoughts 'p', external interferences and distractions 'e', and the now familiar variable of the appropriateness of your state of mind, or level of performance arousal 'a'.

Performance arousal is important

You may think the most amazing thoughts, be physically elite, or be completely unaffected by external distractions, but none of this will matter if your performance arousal level is out of control. Therefore, to optimise your cognitive and physical abilities, and minimise the effects of external interferences, you must achieve an ideal level of performance arousal for your performing situation.

You have the power

Our teachers, mentors, coaches and role models provide the most help in the first part of the equation – cognitive abilities 'c'. Our natural physical attributes 'p' can be enhanced with specific tools or exercises designed to increase our strength, flexibility, and co-ordination. We can go to great lengths to minimise external interferences 'e', for example by checking equipment, ensuring that audience members have mobile phones switched off, and so on.

And just as we have the power to alter these three parts of The Alternative Performance Equation ('c', 'p', and 'e'), we also have the power to alter our performance arousal level ('a'), obtain an ideal state of mind for our performances, and perform in The Zone.

45

Understanding performance arousal and how it affects you and your level of performance is an integral part of understanding The Zone. However the key to actually performing in The Zone is having the ability to exert control over your level of performance arousal. Having the right state of mind for your performance situation – an appropriate level of performance arousal – will give a high value for 'a' in the performance equation, allowing you to achieve a higher resulting level of performance.

Summing up

The techniques and information presented to you here in *Performing in The Zone* can help you to improve the appropriateness of your performance arousal level, allowing you to get closer to realising your full potential as a performer. In controlling your level of performance arousal, you're not only removing performance anxiety or excess excitement. You are in fact focussing and controlling your mind and body, and using the energy you already possess to improve your overall level of performance.

You too can perform in The Zone!

You can learn to enter The Zone – that space, that condition, that state of mind, where everything clicks, where you're unstoppable, where everything is easy, where it all just works, and where you can do nothing but fulfil your true performing potential. In other words, with the right state of mind, you too can **perform in The Zone!**

Afterword

During the time leading up to the research and writing my first thesis *Mind and Body: A Theory for Understanding Levels of Musical Performance* in 2002, I was exploring – seeking out new methods to control my own level of performance arousal so that it could be used to my advantage in performing situations. I still am an explorer with an open mind to new ideas and techniques which may be incorporated into my own performing life, and which may also benefit the performing lives of others.

My journey

At various points along the way, the direction of my own personal journey wasn't always so clear. Today however, now that I have developed and implemented the tools and techniques in this book into my own performing life, I have rediscovered that place I was in as a 13 year old – I have rediscovered how to perform in The Zone. And now with the completion of *Performing in The Zone*, I can say that I have finally figured out exactly where my journey, begun as a 13 year old, has been leading me.

Since the process of writing *Mind and Body: A Theory for Understanding Levels of Musical Performance* began, I have given literally hundreds if not thousands of performances as a soloist, chamber musician, orchestral/opera musician, and public speaker, to literally hundreds of thousands of people around the world. Being able to control my own level of performance arousal has been of immense help to me, especially in situations perceived at the time as being high-pressure.

Rediscovery

Because I've been able to rediscover The Zone, and increase my own level of performance since exploring performance psychology, inventing, defining, refining, adapting, and implementing the techniques in this book, it seemed only appropriate to share these techniques with you, a fellow performer. This to me, is my ultimate way of adding value.

A personal note

It is my wish that in reading this book, you too will make significant progress in controlling your own level of performance arousal. I sincerely hope that the information, exercises, techniques, and complimentary sources of help found in these pages will assist you in getting closer to optimal performance – closer to the place that I like to call, The Zone.

Appendix 1.
Performance Arousal
– How The Zone Diagrams Were Derived

This appendix provides some background information about the process of how the ideas and diagrams shown in Part One of *Performing in The Zone* were derived. The information here has been included as it may prove to be interesting for performers wanting to obtain a deeper understanding of performance arousal, as well as students of performance psychology looking for a starting point for further research in this subject.

Appendix 1 is based heavily on various sections from *Mind and Body: A Theory for Understanding Levels of Performance* as well as *An Explanation of Performance Arousal for Musicians and An Introduction to Suggested Techniques for Control of Performance Arousal.* Both of these texts are available at www.thezonebook.com

Inverted 'U' Theory

The study of the effects of varying levels of psychological activation on performers began at the end of the 19th Century. In 1898, N.D. Triplett observed that cyclists rode faster when racing together than when racing alone.

Triplett's study was followed up in 1908 by the psychologists Yerkes and Dodson, who then derived the 'Inverted 'U' Theory'. This theory proposes that performance is optimal at a moderate level of arousal and progressively declines if arousal increases or decreases (ref. Fig. 1.1). This is supported by Diane Gill's findings that athletes who are too mellow or apathetic give sub par performances[1].

Other studies that support the 'Inverted 'U' Theory' state that problems may arise when an individual becomes over aroused. They suggest that while a moderate level of arousal may be beneficial for performance, higher levels will cause a disintegration of performance.[2] Some more recent studies however have concluded that the inverted 'U' theory is limited, as it does not consider both the positive and negative manifestations of performance arousal (excitement and anxiety).[3]

---

1.   Diane L. Gill, Psychological Dynamics of Sport (Illinois: Human Kinetics Publishers, Inc., 1986), 119.

2.   Hargreaves, Kemp and North, 'Individual Differences - Anxiety', http://www.oxfordmusiconline.com

3   For example, Fazey and Hardy, 1988; Hardy, 1990; Martens et al, 1990.

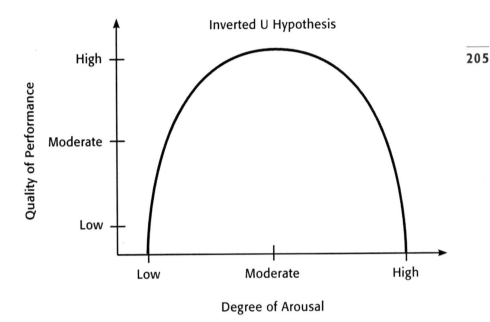

Fig. 1.1 *The inverted 'U' Theory of Performance Arousal vs. Quality of Performance*[4]

4.   After Gill, 119.

The results from various studies, including a specific study of performance arousal in conservatory level music students carried out in 2002 as part of the research process for *Mind and Body: A Theory for Understanding Levels of Musical Performance*, appears to suggest that the inverted 'U' theory is only true when an individual is experiencing the positive manifestation of performance arousal (excitement).[5] A different result seems to stem from the negative manifestation of performance arousal (performance anxiety). The greater the performance arousal level when the negative manifestation is felt, the more negatively affected the performer becomes. (Ref. Fig. 1.2).

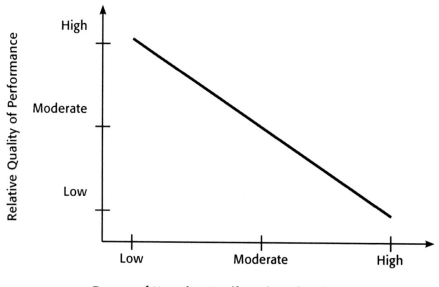

Fig. 1.2 Degree of Negative Manifestation of Performance Arousal vs. Quality of Performance

5. This study incorporated questions on anxiety and excitement, and their perceived effects on performance.

    Refer Mind and Body: A Theory for Understanding Levels of Musical Performance Appendix, pg. 44.

Anxiety and Excitement

In her observation of athletes, Diane Gill has noted the following: "Some sport participants eagerly look forward to competition and thrive on a challenge, whereas others become tense and tentative when faced with intense competition."[6] Those sports people who thrive on challenges experience the positive manifestation of Performance Arousal (excitement) whilst those who become tense during challenges experience the negative manifestation of Performance Arousal (anxiety). This is equally applicable performers of all disciplines.

The study of anxiety in athletes and musicians has generated an extensive literature, much of which relates to controlling the negative manifestation of performance arousal (performance anxiety), whilst neglecting the positive manifestation (excitement, hyped up) almost completely.[7] These studies have shown that anxiety is a highly complex and multifaceted emotion, consisting of 'state' and 'trait' elements.[8]

Trait anxiety can be described as a stable dimension of personality. It is the base level of anxiety against which threats (perceived or real) make their mark. Therefore, an individual with high level of trait anxiety will be more likely to perceive a situation as threatening and will be more prone to panic as a result.

State anxiety, on the other hand, refers to a temporary condition that is produced in response to the immediate perception of a threat. Jones and Hardy give perhaps the most concise definition of anxiety, presenting it as "a multidimensional construct which can be considered from both state and trait perspectives, each of which comprises at least two components: cognitive anxiety and somatic anxiety."[9]

Cognitive anxiety is a psychological response and can include fear of failure, negative thoughts, and general worry. Somatic anxiety is a physical response and can result in such symptoms as sweaty palms, shallow breathing, and nausea.

Excitement, or being 'hyped up', refers to the positive anticipation of an upcoming event. It can aid performance if the level of excitement is appropriate for a given situation. However, it may hinder performance if the level of excitement is inappropriate for a given situation.[10]

---

6. Gill, 55.
7. For example, Stephen Aaron, Stage Fright (Chicago: The University of Chicago Press, 1986); Stuart E. Dunkel, The Audition Process – Anxiety Management and Coping Strategies (New York: Pendragon Press, 1989); Louis Diamant, Psychology of Sports, Exercise, and Fitness – Social and Personal Issues (New York: Hemisphere Publishing Corporation, 1991); John Kremner and Deirdre Scully, Psychology in Sport (London: Taylor and Francis Ltd., 1994).
8. Diamant, Psychology of Sports, Exercise, and Fitness, 51.
9. John Kremner and Deirdre Scully, Psychology in Sport (London: Taylor and Francis Ltd., 1994), 67.
10. This is explained in the section headed Oxendine's Taxonomy.

Excitement, like anxiety, consists of 'state' and 'trait' components. An individual with high trait excitement will find more situations exciting and will be more prone to over-excitement (being 'over-hyped') in situations where there is a high degree of positive anticipation. Excitement also consists of cognitive and somatic components. A graphical explanation of the Positive and Negative Manifestations of Performance Arousal is represented below (ref. fig. 1.3).

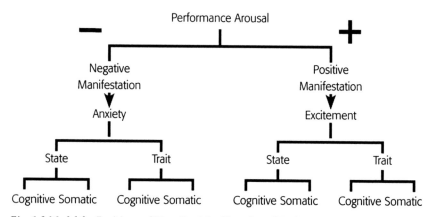

Fig. 1.3 Model for Positive and Negative Manifestation of Performance Arousal

Oxendine's Taxonomy

In 1970, Oxendine argued that an arousal model in regards to performing must take the context of a particular activity into account, namely the demands of specific sports and the tasks associated with that sport.[11] He argued that high levels of excitement are likely to enhance performance tasks involving extreme physical exertion over short periods of time, weightlifting being a prime example. Although beneficial for such intense gross motor tasks, similar high levels of arousal would be detrimental to sports involving complex motor skills, coordination, steadiness, concentration, and fine movement such as golf. Oxendine developed the following taxonomy which endeavoured to place sporting situations alongside relevant levels of arousal (Ref. Fig. 1.4).

11. It is important to understand that Oxendine's Taxonomy is only concerned with the positive manifestation of Performance Arousal (excitement).

OPTIMAL AROUSAL	SPORTING SITUATION
+5	American football blocking; 200/400 metres race; gym exercises; weightlifting
+4	Long jump; sprints/long distance; shot put; swimming races; wrestling/judo
+3	Basketball; boxing; high jump; gymnastics; soccer
+2	Baseball; diving; fencing; tennis
+1	Archery; bowling; golf putting/chipping; figure skating

Fig. 1.4 Oxendine's Taxonomy of Sport[12]

Oxendine's observations suggest that in a positive manifestation of Performance Arousal, the peak of the inverted 'U' is not fixed, but rather changes depending upon the performance situation. Certain performance situations may require a high level of arousal for the performer to feel in The Zone whereas other situations may require a low level of arousal for the performer to feel in The Zone. A graphical representation of Oxendine's ideas is depicted in fig. 1.5.

12. Kremner and Scully, 64

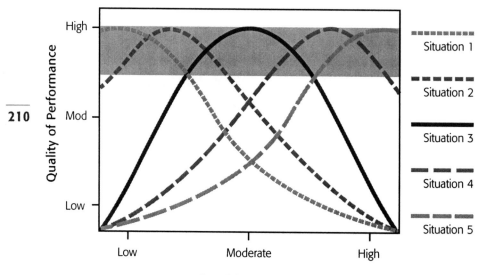

Fig. 1.5 Inverted 'U' Theory – Modified by Oxendine's Taxonomy

The inverted 'U' Theory, modified by Oxendine's Taxonomy, as in fig. 1.5, can be applied to any performance situation, as shown in, fig. 1.6.

OPTIMAL AROUSAL	PERFORMING SITUATION
+5	Actor – playing the role of a hysterical psychopath
+4	Dancer – street dance demonstration
+3	Public speaker – motivating an audience
+2	Violinist – playing solo recital
+1	Golfer – putting

Fig. 1.6 Taxonomy of Performance

Appendix 2. Performance Journal

Step 1: Practise Performing in Your Mind

Day/Date/Time _____

Location _____

Up-coming performance _____

Performance arousal level(s) required _____

Performance arousal level(s) experienced _____

Techniques utilised _____

_____

_____

_____

Noted positive effects _____

_____

What did I do well? _____

_____

What can I improve? _____

_____

Notes

_____

_____

_____

_____

_____

_____

_____

Step 2: Practise Performing by Yourself

Day/Date/Time _____

Location _____

Up-coming performance _____

Performance arousal level(s) required _____

Performance arousal level(s) experienced _____

Techniques utilised _____

_____

_____

_____

Noted positive effects _____

_____

What did I do well? _____

_____

What can I improve? _____

_____

Notes

_____

_____

_____

_____

_____

_____

_____

_____

_____

Step 3: Practise Performing to a Recording Device

Day/Date/Time _____

Location _____

Up-coming performance _____

Performance arousal level(s) required _____

Performance arousal level(s) experienced _____

Techniques utilised _____

_____

_____

_____

Noted positive effects _____

_____

What did I do well? _____

_____

What can I improve? _____

_____

Notes

_____

_____

_____

_____

_____

_____

_____

_____

Step 4: Practise Performing to Close Friends or Colleagues

Day/Date/Time _____

Location _____

Up-coming performance _____

Performance arousal level(s) required _____

Performance arousal level(s) experienced _____

Techniques utilised _____

_____

_____

_____

Noted positive effects _____

_____

What did I do well? _____

_____

What can I improve? _____

_____

Notes

_____

_____

_____

_____

_____

_____

_____

Step 5: Practising Performing

Day/Date/Time _____

Location _____

Up-coming performance _____

Performance arousal level(s) required _____

Performance arousal level(s) experienced _____

Techniques utilised _____

_____

_____

_____

Noted positive effects _____

_____

What did I do well? _____

_____

What can I improve? _____

_____

Notes

_____

_____

_____

_____

_____

_____

_____

_____

Bibliography and Suggested Further Reading

Books and articles

Aaron, Stephen
Stage fright
Chicago: The University of Chicago Press, 1986.

Alcantara, Pedro de.
Indirect Procedures –
A Musicians Guide to the Alexander Technique
Oxford: Clarendon Press, 1997.

Alexander, F.M.
Bedre Brug af Sig Selv
(The Use of the Self)
Aarhus: Novis Publications, 1995.
(London: Victor Gollancz, 1985)

Angelöw, B.
Meditera för ett Bättre Liv – Om Transcendental Meditation
Stockholm: Graphic Systems, 1993.

Armstrong, J.
Never Ask Why – The Life Experience of Kitty Wielopolska
Aarhus: Novis Publications, 2001.

Bragg, Paul C, and Bragg, Patricia
Bragg Healthy Lifestyle
Vital Living to 120
Santa Barbara: Health Science, 2004.

Bragg, Paul C, and Bragg, Patricia
The Miracle of Fasting
Santa Barbara: Health Science, 2004.

Carlson, Neil R. William Buskist and Neil G. Martin.
Psychology – The Science of Behaviour
Harlow: Pearson Education Ltd., 2000.

Carlson, Richard
Stop Thinking and Start Living
London: HarperCollins Publishers, 2003

Carron, Albert V.
Social Psychology of Sport
New York: Mouvement Publications, 1980

Chadwick, Felicia.   **Beyond Belief – Talent Development in Music**
                       Newcastle: University of Newcastle, 2001.

Dahl, Ole Vadum   **Grund Bog i NLP**
                       I. Kommunikation og Terapi
                       København: Paludan, 1993

Davis, Richard   **Becoming an Orchestral Musician**
                       London: Giles de la Mare Publishers Ltd, 2004.

Deutsch, Diana, ed.   **The Psychology of Music**
                       New York: Academic Press Ltd., 1982.

Diamant, Louis, ed.   **Psychology of Sports, Exercise, and Fitness –**
                       Social and Personal Issues
                       New York: Hemisphere Publishing Corporation, 1991.

Ding, Master John.   **15-Minute Tai Chi: Strong Body, Still Mind**
                       London: Thorsons, 2003.

Dunkel, Stuart E.   **The Audition Process –**
                       Anxiety Management and coping strategies
                       New York: Pendragon Press, 1989.

Einstein, Albert   **Ideas and Opinions**
                       New York: The Three Rivers Press, 1995.

Einstein, Albert   **The World as I see it**
                       Minneapolis: Filiquarian Publishing, LLC., 2007.

Enhager, K.   **Kvantgolf - Nytändning för Frustrerade Golfare**
                       Helsingborg: Schmidts Boktrykeri, 1992.

Fiske, Harold E.   **Music Cognition and Aesthetic Attitudes**
                       Dyfed: The Edwin Mellen Press, 1993.

Floyd, Angeleita S. "Finding Balance: Position, Posture, and Presentation", The Flutist's Handbook: A Pedagogy Anthology. Article excerpted from Chapter 3, "Principles of Fundamental Technique" of The Gilbert Legacy by Angeleita S. Floyd. Winzer Press, 1994.

218 Freeman, Eric and Freeman, Elisabeth **Head First Design Patterns A Brain-Friendly Guide** Sebastopol: O'Reilly Media, Inc., 2004

Freymuth, M. **Mental Practice and Imagery for Musicians** Boulder: Integrated Musician's Press, 1999.

Gallwey, T. **The Inner Game of Tennis** New York: Random House, 1974.

Gerzabek, Ute. **The Power of Breathing** London: Marshall Publishing, 1999.

Gill, Diane L. **Psychological Dynamics of Sport** Illinois: Human Kinetics Publishers, Inc., 1986.

Godøy, Rolf Inge & Harald Jørgenson, eds. **Musical Imagery** Lisse: Swets & Zeitlinger Publishers, 2001.

Gordon, C. **Systematic Approach to Daily Practice for Trumpet** New York: Carl Fischer, 1968.

Gorrie, J. **An Explanation of Performance Arousal for Musicians and An Introduction to Suggested Techniques for Control of Performance Arousal** Gothenburg: Gothenburg University, 2005.

Gorrie, J. **Just another day at the office...** Gothenburg: Gothenburg University, 2005.

Gorrie, J. **Mind and Body: A Theory for Understanding Levels of Musical Performance** Wellington: Victoria University of Wellington, 2002.

Green, Barry and   **The Inner Game of Music**
T. Gallwey   New York: Doubleday & Co., Inc., 1986.

Greene, D.   **Audition Success – An Olympic Sports Psychologist**
                       Teaches Performing Artists How to Win
                       New York: Routledge, 2001.

Grindea, C. ed.   **Tensions in the Performance of Music**
                       London: Kahn and Averill, 1978.

Hewstone, M.,   **Introduction to Social Psychology**
W. Stroebe, and   Oxford: Blackwell Publishers Ltd., 1996.
G.M. Stephenson, eds.

Hickman, D.   **Trumpet Lessons with David Hickman**
                       Volume V – Psychology of Performance
                       Denver: Tromba, 1989.

Hollingworth, H.L.   **The Psychology of the Audience**
                       New York: American Book Company, 1935.

Jones, C.   **What Makes Winners Win**
                       New York: Broadway Books, 1997.

Kremner, J and   **Psychology in Sport**
D. Scully.   London: Taylor and Francis Ltd., 1994.

Kryter, K.D.   **Handbook of Hearing and the Effects of Noise**
                       New York: Academic Press, 1996.

Lieberman, J.L.   **You Are Your Instrument**
                       New York: Huiksi Music, 1997

Marks, Isaac M.   **Living with Fear – Understanding and Coping with Anxiety**
                       London: McGraw-Hill Publishing Company, 1978.

219

Masterson, J.F.   Det Truede Selv (The Search for the Real Self)
                   Borderline og narcissisme –
                   Personlighedsforstyrrelser i det moderne samfund
                   Gylling: Narayana Press, 1990.

Mayland, E.L.   Rosen Method: An Approach to Wholeness and Well-Being
                  Through the Body
                  Santa Cruz: 52 Stone Press, 2005.

Orlick, T.   In Pursuit of Excellence – How to Win in Sport and Life
                  through Mental Training
                  Champaign IL: Human Kinetics, 2000.

Railo, W.   Nya Bäst När Det Gäller – Idrottspsykologi
                  Sverige: Skogs Grafiska AB, 1992.

Reid, D.   A Complete Guide to Chi-Gung
                  Boston: Shambala Publications Inc. 1998.

Reid, D.   The Tao of Health, Sex and Longevity
                  New York: Fireside – Simon and Schuster, 1989.

Reid, D.,   The Complete Book of Chinese Health and Healing:
Chou, D., and   Guarding the Three Treasures
Huang, J.   Boston: Shambala Publications Inc. 1994.

Reid, D.   Traditional Chinese Medicine
                  Boston: Shambala Publications Inc. 1996.

Seashore, Carl E. Psychology of Music
                   New York: Dover Publications Inc., 1967.

Seashore, Carl E. Psychology of Musical Talent
                   Boston: Silver, Burdett and Co., 1919.

Shaffer, David, R. Developmental Psychology – Studenthood and Adolescence
                    New York : Brooks/Cole Publishing Company, 1999.

Snell, H.   The Trumpet – Its Practice and Performance
                             Brighouse: Kirklees Music, 1997.

Spilling, M. ed.   Handbook of the Human Body
                             London: Amber Books Ltd., 2006.

Toff, Nancy.   The Flute Book – A Complete Guide for   **221**
                             Students and Performers
                             London: Oxford University Press, 1996.

Tolle, Eckhart.   The Power of Now
                             A Guide to Spiritual Enlightenment
                             London: Hodder and Stoughton. 1999.

Tze, Lao.   Tao Teh Ching
Trans. Wu, J. C. H.   Boston: Shambala Publications Inc., 2005.

Tzu, Sun   The Art of War
                             Boston: Shambala Publications Inc., 1991.

Ungerleider, S.   Mental Training for Peak Performance
                             Emmaus, Pennsylvania: Rosedale Press, Inc. 1996.

Vaughn, M and   Introduction to Social Psychology – 2nd Edition
Hogg, Michael A.   Victoria: McPhersons Printing Group, 1998.

Werner, K.   Effortless Mastery
                             Liberating the Master Musician Within
                             New Albany: Jamey Aebersold Jazz, Inc., 1996.

Wilson, Paul.   The Quiet: Four Simple Steps to Peace and Contentment
                             – Without Spending Your Life on a Mountaintop
                             London: MacMillan, 1997.

Zi, Nancy.   The Art of Breathing
                             New York: Bantam Books, Inc., 1986.

Online and electronic resources

American Speech-Language-Hearing Association.	**Noise** www.asha.org
ARA Content.	**The Mind-Body Benefits of Physical Fitness** www.mamashealth.com/exercise/mindbody.asp
Arnold, Joan.	**Poise in Performance: Alexander Technique for Musicians** www.alexandertechnique.com/articles/musicians
Berk, Dr. Lee and Tan, Dr. Stanley.	**The Benefits of Laughter** www.holisticonline.com/Humor_Therapy/humor_therapy_benefits.htm
Clarke, Eric F.	**Psychology of music – Performance** www.oxfordmusiconline.com
Cross, Ian.	**Psychology of music – History – The late 20th Century** www.oxfordmusiconline.com
Geary, Amanda.	**The Mind guide to food and mood** www.mind.org.uk
Gordon, Claude.	**The Seven Natural Elements of Brass Playing** www.claudegordonmusic.com
Hargreaves, David, Anthony Kemp and Adrian North.	**Psychology of music – Social Psychology** www.oxfordmusiconline.com
Kataria, Dr. Madan.	**Laughter Clubs** www.laughteryoga.org
LaLanne, Jack.	**The Jack LaLanne Show and other DVDs** www.jacklalanne.com
Lewcock, Ronald, Rijn Pirn, and Jürgen Meyer.	**Acoustics – Room Acoustics** www.oxfordmusiconline.com
Lewis, Dennis.	**Breathing Tips and Research for Health, Well Being and Inner Growth** www.breathing.com
Lundeberg, Åke.	**The Art of Performing Under Pressure** user.tninet.se/pdi969s/york.htm
National Geographic.	**My Brilliant Brain** www1.natgeochannel.co.uk/explore/MyBrilliantBrain

222

Nausbaum, Nora. **What is the Difference between the Alexander Technique and Feldenkrais Method?**
www.ati-net.com

Neimark, N. **The Fight or Flight Response**
www.thebodysoulconnection.com/EducationCenter/fight.html

O'Neill, Susan. **Psychology of music – Musical Ability**
www.oxfordmusiconline.com

Robbins, Anthony. **Get the Edge**
www.tonyrobbins.com

Robbins, Anthony. **Personal Power 2**
www.tonyrobbins.com

Schacherer, Nathan. **Voice projection and tone**
www.socialsupermen.com

Shakya, Grandmaster Jy Din. **Empty Cloud – The Teachings of Xu Yun**
www.jcrows.com/XuYunTeachings.html

Spurlock, Morgan. **Super Size Me**
www.imdb.com/title/tt0390521/

Szabo, Billet and Turner **Phenylethylamine: A Possible Link to the Antidepressant**
www.bjsm.bmj.com   **Effects of Exercise?**

Tolle, Eckhart. **Practising the Power of Now**
www.eckharttolle.com

Tolle, Eckhart. **The Power of Not Knowing**
www.eckharttolle.com

Toms, Justine Willis. **The Art of Breathing**
www.justinewillistoms.com

Wikipedia **Body Mass Index**   en.wikipedia.org/wiki/Body_mass_index
Haile Gebrselassie   en.wikipedia.org/wiki/Haile_Gebrselassie
Hypothalamus   en.wikipedia.org/wiki/Hypothalamus
Neuro-linguistic Programming
en.wikipedia.org/wiki/Neuro-linguistic_programming
Qigong   en.wikipedia.org/wiki/Qigong

About the author

Jon Gorrie (b.1977)

Originally from New Zealand, Jon Gorrie was taught the art of classical trumpet playing by several renowned master teachers including John (Jack) Lauderdale and Howard Snell. His musical endeavours have taken him to all four corners of the world with solo, chamber, orchestral, and operatic performances in recent years in Sweden, Denmark, Norway and Iceland.

Jon is a professional trumpet player, conductor, composer/arranger, brass pedagogue, and mental trainer/coach with many student success stories. He has also been active as an educational advisor for institutions of higher learning.

Jon is fluent in English, Swedish, and Norwegian, reads Danish, and has the following formal qualifications and titles:

BMus	Bachelor of Music, Auckland University.
PGdip(RNCM)	Post-Graduate diploma in advanced studies in musical performance, Royal Northern College of Music.
MMus(distinction)	Master of Music in Performance, passed with Distinction, Victoria University of Wellington.
MOrchStud	Master of Orchestral Studies, Swedish National Orchestra Academy.
FTCL	Fellow of Trinity College London.